The Art
of Coaching
Track and Field

Ken Brauman

Parker Publishing Company, Inc.
West Nyack, New York

© 1986 *by*
PARKER PUBLISHING COMPANY, INC.
West Nyack, N.Y.

Library of Congress Cataloging-in-Publication Data

Brauman, Ken.
    The art of coaching track and field.

    Includes index.
        1. Track-athletics—United States—Coaching.
I. Title.
GV1060.675.C6B73   1986   796.4'2'0973   85-29784

ISBN 0-13-046640-9

Printed in the United States of America

THIS BOOK IS DEDICATED TO THE LOVING
MEMORY OF MY MOTHER AND FATHER
ELLA MARIE BABCOCK BRAUMAN
December 20, 1920–November 1, 1972
KENNETH WILLIS BRAUMAN
December 30, 1919–September 24, 1983

How This Book Will Help You

In high school track and field, you, the coach, must wear many hats. Not only are you responsible for the training of the athlete, but you must also do the scheduling, planning for large scale competitions, maintaining the track facility, and even acting as a father figure for many of your athletes.

Even though university coaching programs prepare you for the technical aspects of coaching, they often neglect the administrative and emotional aspects. These areas are left for you to master through years of trial and error experimentation.

The Art of Coaching Track and Field will help you, the high school coach, to gain knowledge and insight into these areas through the experiences of a highly successful high school coach.

In essence, this book is about everything that you should have been taught in college but weren't.

A wise man once wrote that the average coach teaches a sport to young people, while the successful coach teaches young people a sport.

This book will help to organize your philosophy of athletics by helping you to determine and define your values, goals, and overall feelings toward young people and sports. After all, your philosophy is the entire justification for your program and it will determine the ultimate success or failure of your program.

A major goal in any athletic program is to have as many members on the team as possible. *The Art of Coaching Track and Field* will help you to expand your program by suggesting various time-tested and highly successful methods for promoting your program on both the community and school level. This book will provide you with ideas for encouraging students to participate in your program and for keeping them interested by selecting the correct events and giving them an incentive for success.

The success of the program can only be measured by its organization. This book will help you to become a better organized coach by showing you how to use your time more wisely and suggesting shortcuts, through organization, in planning and conducting large scale competitions. It will show you how to improve these competitions and use them as a positive public relations tool for expanding your program.

This manual will also offer you timesaving suggestions for the preparation and upkeep of your facility to make it a showcase for your school, your community, and your program.

How a skill is presented to a young person determines to a large extent how quickly it will be learned. This book will offer you proven and successful methods for dealing with young people on an individual basis when teaching a skill. It will also help you to determine and establish a training philosophy so that you will be better prepared to deal with young athletes at their various levels of skill development by establishing a competitive philosophy based on this level of skill development.

The United States Olympic Committee for Track and Field has defined three areas of concentration for their sport:

1. Physiological
2. Biomechanical
3. Psychological

The physiological and biomechanical aspects of track and field are exact sciences and are taught to prospective coaches on the university level.

The psychological aspect of this sport is considered more of an art than a science. In this area you are dealing with the intangibles of the human mind. What motivates an individual to run, jump, and throw faster and farther than ever before? What causes an athlete in superb physical condition to completely fail in a race? What roles do tension and relaxation play in the success or failure of an individual?

These questions and more will be answered in *The Art of Coaching Track and Field.* In addition, you will discover various methods of controlling anxiety and preparing your athletes for competition through the use of mental discipline and various competitive tactics.

This book has broader vision than other manuals on track and field. It deals with the athlete as an individual, his self-concept, values, goals, and his uniqueness and worth as an individual in determining if winning is everything.

The Art of Coaching Track and Field reflects the author's experience with bridging the gap between the coach, the athlete, the community, and the school while molding a highly successful and competitive track and field program.

K.B.

Contents

1

You As a Coach— The Importance of a Sound Coaching Philosophy

Coaching is both the art and science of teaching through sports. As an art, it requires knowledge and effort, and as a science, it is based on sound scientific truths. In many respects, it is the most challenging of all professions because you must deal with the total individual: the physical, mental, emotional, social, and spiritual nature of the person. It requires skill, study, observation, creativity, understanding, ingenuity, persuasiveness, and the ability to explain, to make simple, to adapt, and never to be satisfied with your results. It is further compounded by the fact that each and every athlete is a unique individual and no one method of coaching is best. You may have fifty team members and have to employ fifty different methods for working with each individual in order to maximize each athlete's potential.

The foundation for all that you do is a sound philosophy of coaching. This philosophy should determine your aims and objectives and be the basis for all of your decisions. Your philosophy is the most important determinant for successful coaching.

The basis for this philosophy is your own morals and values. These values are learned from your parents, peers, teachers, coaches, church, society, and even the media. Once this value system has been established, a moral code is formed and with it a sense of self-identity: a sense of knowing who you are, what is important to you, and where you are going in life. This value system and moral code are the foundations for establishing the goals and objectives you will use to conduct and build an effective and successful program.

In essence, *success* should be the key word and ultimate goal of all athletic programs. Success, not winning. Only one team can win a contest. Only one individual can win a race. Does this mean that those who did not win are failures? No. Winning is the ultimate goal of all individuals whether it be in athletics, business, or any other facet of the real world, but, is winning everything? No. What of the individual who improves one minute in the two-mile run during the course of a season and never places in a race. Is that person a failure? As long as he works to constantly become better—a better athlete, a better person—then the program that fosters this attitude is a successful program. Successful coaches and successful programs achieve more than just winning. They are holistic in nature because they deal with the development of the entire individual, the individual's physical, mental, emotional, social, and moral development. The successful coach stresses that becoming is far superior to being. The individual should be striving constantly toward becoming a better athlete, a better student, a better person, not just finishing in first place. The successful person is one who is struggling constantly to become more successful. With that success will eventually come winning. For in all of life, don't you derive satisfaction more from the struggle, the self-sacrifice, the striving, than from achieving the goal itself?

One person alone controls the quality of the program: *you, the coach.* What you do, what you say, how you handle yourself, will determine how the team will perform, react, and handle themselves. You, maybe more than anyone else, have the power to influence and shape the lives of so many impressionable young people. There is an old saying: "you teach the way you are taught and you live your life the way you have been taught to live it." The lives of so many young people throughout the years have been influenced and shaped entirely by their coach's concept of self, his value system, and his moral code. It is an awesome responsibility.

WHO IS THE SUCCESSFUL COACH

There are many coaches throughout the nation who have the knowledge necessary to teach young athletes the proper techniques for each sport. Why, then, are some coaches more successful than others? Why are some programs more successful than others? Why don't we have many more successful programs throughout the nation?

In the hallways of every school walks the material for a State Championship team in some sport. True, some areas are blessed with more talent than others and some areas have a better climate for training than others. However, the driving force behind every successful program is the coach who not only has the scientific knowledge for teaching technique but also has mastered the art of dealing with human beings.

What are the special qualities that set the successful coach apart from all others?

- Warmth
- Respect
- Success
- Honesty
- Knowledge

WARMTH

1. Whenever possible, each athlete should be welcomed and spoken to in a genuine and positive manner before and after each practice and competition.

2. You should tell each athlete "goodbye" at the end of each practice session and competition in a way that makes him feel wanted, accepted, and eager to return the next day. A simple "pat on the back" will do far more for an individual's self-concept and security than anything else.

3. Share your feelings with each athlete. Laughter, anger, excitement, and enthusiasm are all vehicles for informing the athlete that you are a human being and are responsive to all facets of his personality.

4. Notice and comment favorably on the things that are important to each athlete. New clothes, a new car, and

better grades are just a few examples of things that may be important to the athlete. Each athlete should feel that you have a genuine interest not only in what happens on the athletic field but off it as well.

5. Give special attention to each athlete every day, even if it is just a pat on the back, a handshake, or saying "good job." Each athlete should feel that note of encouragement from you; that you have paid special and specific attention to him during a practice session. Know when their birthdays are and express your congratulations for accomplishments in all areas.

6. Express an interest in each athlete's family. Ask how brothers and sisters are feeling, how parents are getting along at their jobs. Become interested in the entire family and express your acceptance of that family no matter what their socioeconomic level.

7. Spend time with each athlete off the field as well as on. Eat lunch, converse with each one at ball games or when you see them at the supermarket or game room. Talk about outside activities and events that are important, not just the sport itself.

8. Encourage the athlete to expand and become more involved in other worthwhile areas of life, not just sports.

9. Have empathy for the athlete. Be able to place yourself in each athlete's situation. Try to understand what each athlete is feeling during victory and defeat and remember that no matter how an individual reacts to defeat or a mistake, no one feels any worse about it than he does.

10. Accept each athlete both in victory and in defeat. The most important aspect in any competition is not the winning or losing but being able to walk off the field knowing that you tried.

11. Above all, be able to accept each and every individual as a unique, and worthwhile member of society with the ability to contribute to society in a positive manner

regardless of race, physical appearance, physical ability, or socioeconomic background.

RESPECT

The respect that your athletes show you must be earned, not demanded. Each athlete must willingly give of himself to you and your program because he perceives you as a warm, caring individual, not a dictator who uses force and scare tactics to get cooperation.

1. Learn each athlete's name as soon as possible. Learn where they live and who their parents, brothers, and sisters are. You cannot adequately deal with the whole person unless you know how that individual functions and the reasons behind his day-to-day actions.

2. Talk *with* not *at* the athlete. It is important for the athlete to know that what is being said is being said directly to him. Much more can be accomplished when the athlete has this feeling of being special.

3. Be patient with the athlete. Not everyone develops at the same rate. The slower developing individuals should be given as much assistance and encouragement as the elite athlete. Who knows, maybe in a few years, the 95-pound weakling will turn out to be 6'5", 180 pounds, and run the 100-meter in 10.3 seconds. Provide each athlete with an atmosphere that is conducive to feeling accepted without the "do-or-die" pressure.

4. Don't be a dictator. Allow the athlete to have a voice in planning workouts and in establishing team rules. Show a special interest in all observations that each individual makes and encourage new and innovative activities and ideas. Open the lines and encourage two-way communication.

5. Allow the athlete to challenge your opinions, but never your authority. This will promote critical thinking

and analysis. Always be prepared to defend and explain the reasons for everything you do, but never discourage the athlete from questioning those principles. If you don't know why you do something, the athletes will never have confidence in you to direct an adequate development program for them.

6. Always allow the athlete the opportunity to demonstrate his ability. Never take for granted what an athlete can or cannot do without first observing him in fair competition. Never "outmatch" an athlete. The more equal the competition, the more competitive the individual and the more valid your assessment of that individual's abilities will be.

7. Avoid excessive criticism of the individual and be generous in your praise of each person. Abusive or negative comments serve only to embarrass an athlete and lower his self-esteem. The athlete who is treated this way will never reach the ultimate level of development.

8. Practice real and honest courtesy with each individual. Treat him as you yourself would want to be treated. Better yet, treat each athlete as though he were your own child. You can be stern and demanding while at the same time being warm and caring. When the athletes perceive that your criticism is being communicated in a constructive, warm, and caring manner, their resistance to change will be minimal.

9. Keep in mind the maturity level of the individuals with whom you are working. They cannot all be the fully developed, highly motivated, goal-oriented people we would like to deal with. Look at each individual and see what he can become, not what he is now. Begin now to lay the ground work for future development by working with each athlete at a pace commensurate with his maturity level.

10. Practice what you preach. Do not be hypocritical and stress one thing while doing just the opposite yourself.

If you talk about the evils of drugs and alcohol, be courageous enough not to become involved in their use yourself. How can you gain the respect of an athlete if you encourage him to keep his body highly tuned, but you, yourself, are overweight and miserably out of shape.

SUCCESS

To become successful year after year, a program must have new athletes coming up and developing through the grades. You cannot just concentrate on a few highly skilled upperclassmen because they will be gone the following year. Part of success in developing athletes lies in numbers. The more students you can recruit to come out and stay out for your program, the greater your chances are of assuring an adequate number of athletes year-in and year-out. In order to secure the participation of a large number of athletes, you must work with each and every one, and encourage them all, through competition, to remain in your program.

1. Make sure that each athlete has a reasonable chance to succeed by providing the proper instruction, by spending time with each, and by providing regular competition at various skill levels to accommodate each athlete. This will keep them interested and involved in your program all year.

2. Take the opportunity to reward and praise each athlete regardless of his level of development. Make sure you give support and encouragement to the slower developing athletes. This can be accomplished through positive remarks and a general concern for each one.

3. A method for securing the continued hard work and loyalty of the athlete is to set tasks and workouts that are within his ability range. Nothing is more discouraging for an individual than to attempt something he cannot possibly complete. The tasks must be interesting, challenging, enjoyable, and within reach for successful completion.

4. In addition to being attainable, all tasks and competitions should be honest experiences. They should not be manufactured or fabricated to give the athlete a false sense of accomplishment.

5. Allow each athlete the opportunity to make mistakes without penalty so that he can learn a lesson from each one. If someone is afraid to make a mistake for fear of punishment, he will invariably commit far more mistakes than the normal individual. An athlete should not fear mistakes but learn from them in order to become a better person.

6. Recognize the progress of each individual. An athlete still may not have the ability to be a top member of the team, but may have improved dramatically throughout the season or since the previous year. This individual should be given as much, if not more, recognition and encouragement as any star on the team. Always compare where they were to where they are now.

7. Give each athlete an opportunity to be trustworthy by delegating responsibility. Every person, even the most undesirable, craves the chance to be a trusted member of an organization. From this trust, a genuine feeling of self-importance and accomplishment will evolve. The better a person feels about himself, the more motivated he will become to excel.

8. Know the difference between ability and attitude. Know how far each athlete can travel on the road to improvement. Keep challenging him until he has reached that ability level.

HONESTY

1. Don't lie to an athlete or for an athlete. Lying will only confuse the athlete as to where you stand morally and will hurt his own self-image in the final analysis. Fabricated times or distances in order to secure good heat and lane assignments will only embarrass the athlete

when he cannot live up to those marks in actual competition.

2. Be yourself at all times. Phonies never last long in this profession. Young people will pick up any insincerity on your part in no time and you will lose any respect they may have had for you. You can be the person and the coach you train yourself to be.

3. Try to conduct yourself in a level-headed manner. Don't go berzerk when something goes wrong. Show your athletes that you are an individual who can handle any circumstance in a truly professional manner.

4. Avoid having "favorites" or "victims." Convey the feeling that all athletes are equally important.

5. Admit your strengths and weaknesses as a person and continue to work toward becoming a better individual.

6. Have a clear idea of what is and what is not acceptable in your program. Convey this to each athlete.

7. If some form of punishment is unavoidable, make sure it is positive, not degrading. Ridiculous and humiliating forms of punishment will only turn the athlete off to your program. The punishment should fit the offense and once it is imposed, make sure it is carried out. This punishment should be fair and apply to everyone.

8. Remember to accept and understand small discipline problems. They are a form of human nature for the young person and should not be taken as personal insults. Within limits, there is room for the athlete to be both active and natural.

9. Arrive at each practice session before the athletes. Be thoroughly prepared for the session. Leave only after the athletes have completed their workouts and have gone.

10. The integrity of your program will be based on your honesty and moral conduct.

KNOWLEDGE

An important factor in being able to deal with or manage young people is securing their loyalty and unwavering belief that what you are saying is true. Once you can convince the athlete to believe you, ninety-nine percent of the battle is won. The only way to secure this faith is to command the knowledge necessary to teach sound, scientific technique in such a manner that the athlete can easily grasp and understand it.

1. You should be drill-oriented. There is nothing more important in the preparation of an individual than the extensive and efficient use of drills. These drills must accurately simulate the actual movements involved in a specific event. They should also teach the individual how to react correctly under competitive conditions.

Know the reasons "why" for each drill and be able to communicate these reasons to the athlete. If an athlete wants to know the value of doing something, give a clear, concise, and true explanation.

2. Be thorough in your teaching and teach the finer points of each event. Give the athlete additional confidence by stressing that he is a cut above everyone else because of the knowledge you have given him.

3. You must be goal oriented. Your program should have both long-range and immediate goals. You need a design for each athlete and a design for the entire program. These goals have to be attainable. If you don't set proper goals, your program will have no direction and each team member will flounder.

4. Work to improve yourself as a teacher and a motivator. The one factor that separates a good teacher from a mediocre teacher is the ability to transmit knowledge to another person. How can you become a better teacher?

- Know exactly what you want to teach and how you want to teach it.
- Learn how to convey your thoughts clearly to all members of the team, not just your best athletes.
- Be yourself.
- Constantly evaluate your teaching procedures. Search for new and more effective methods to convey your material to the athletes.

5. If you have confidence in your program, so will the athletes. Avoid change for the sake of change. Everything you do must be well thought-out and clearly compatible with the goals and objectives of your program. Don't change your progam in the middle of the season. This will only lead to confusion and mistrust on the part of the athlete. The season is a time for doing. Off-season is the time for analysis and change. Don't be afraid to subject your program to a critical analysis. Try not to confuse stubborn unwillingness to change with faith in your program. You should learn something each season and become wiser in the methods for dealing with the athlete. Use this wisdom to improve your program.

6. You must sell your program and your knowledge to the athlete. Don't be afraid to admit you make mistakes, but let the athlete know that your program is a well thought-out, viable system through which he can attain success. The athlete must believe in you and your program.

7. There will be times—some more severe than others—when you feel that nothing is going the way you planned. You will be tempted to react in ways that are not consistent with your character. Just remember that all teams go through a time of unusual difficulty. The athletes will be watching closely to see how you handle yourself during these periods of stress. Their reactions will be based on your reaction. You can either solidify your

position as a leader, or completely lose control over the team. If you are confident that what you are doing is correct, then you will overcome all obstacles.

8. A coach is like a champion athlete. You should exhibit the same competitive attitude, aiming toward becoming the best. Your program and your actions should exhibit high standards of excellence.

9. Know the difference between ability and attitude in an athlete. Encourage maximum development, but don't expect each one to become a state champion.

10. Remember that the less background and knowledge you have in a sport, the more important *conditioning* becomes. An athlete in sound physical condition can often defeat a more highly skilled athlete who is not in as good condition.

In order to become successful, you must be a guidance counselor as well as a coach. You must be able to direct, suggest, motivate, and inspire the athlete to develop the attributes of self-discipline, self-sacrifice, and the will to succeed. These are attributes that cannot be drilled into an individual, they must be cultivated until the athlete feels that everything that happens is a result of his superior performance, not because of you. These attributes come from within each person. Each athlete must make the decision to either succeed or fail. The information on which this decision is based will be gleaned from you. Your values, morals, personality, attitude, and philosophy as perceived by the athlete determine if that athlete will make a commitment to excellence. You are the role model from which the athlete will develop. If you are constantly striving to become a better coach, your athletes will strive to improve themselves. You and your philosophy can make the difference between success and failure.

2

Program Organization and Management

Once your philosophy has been defined, you can formulate a plan for the administrative organization of your program. First impressions are very important. If an athlete feels that your program is organized effectively on all points, he will have a more secure feeling. If you don't know what you are doing on a day-to-day basis; if you say one thing and do another; if you don't have a systematic organization that takes into account any eventuality; your athletes will not be confident that what you are doing is correct.

TEAM MANAGEMENT

You can have proper organization and management only when common purposes and actions are shared. Management is the coordination of thoughts and actions around a shared purpose.

1. The first priority of organization and management is to serve the greatest interest of the team, promoting their greatest fulfillment as individuals. If you become concerned with everything that is happening in each athlete's life you will recognize and understand his thought processes, know when and how much material he can absorb, and know when he is experiencing difficulties that might inhibit learning or training. A superior amount of stewardship will allow you to establish an environment in which your athletes can flourish.

2. Time management is undoubtedly the number one concern of all coaches. How can you complete all that you need to in the time allowed? This becomes even more critical when you spend time in the classroom and then are expected to run an efficient practice after school. Here are some suggestions for more efficient management of your time.

• Set up a deadline for every goal.

- Do not trust your memory. Write down everything that you want to accomplish by the end of the day, week, or month.
- Be aware of your priorities so that you will not waste a great deal of time on something that is not that important.
- Improve your reading skills. If you can go through material quickly and still maintain a high level of comprehension, you will become more effective in time management.
- Delegate tasks to your assistant(s) coach(es) and manager(s) if they can handle them effectively. It is impossible for you to do everything.
- Find a fool-proof reminder system, such as a desk calendar, that you will be sure to look at each day. Keep your "things to do" list on this calendar.
- Consolidate your activities whenever possible. Handle all correspondence at one specific time, all telephone calls at another, etc.
- Establish an effective filing system and keep it up to date. This filing system should contain:

(1). ADMINISTRATION
- 1a. Accident/injury reports.
- 1b. Physical forms.
- 1c. Parent permission forms.
- 1d. Insurance identification on each athlete.
- 1e. Class schedules and information sheets for each athlete.
- 1f. Competitive schedules from the previous five years.
- 1g. Meet contracts.
- 1h. School activity calendar.
- 1i. Job descriptions for the head coach, assistant coach, and team manager.

1j. Team Policies.
  1j-1. Awards.
  1j-2. Eligibility rules.
  1j-3. Facilities use.
  1j-4. Lettering system.
  1j-5. Training rules.
1k. Team Handbook.
1l. National and state rule books.

(2). ASSOCIATIONS
  2a. State high school athletic coaches association.
  2b. National High School Coaches Association.
  2c. Fellowship of Christian Athletes.
  2d. NCAA recruiting regulations.
  2e. NJCAA recruiting regulations.
  2f. NAIA recruiting regulations.
  2g. Conference rules and regulations.

(3). LIBRARY
  3a. Books and magazines on track and field available in the school and public library.
  3b. Films and videos available at the school media center.

(4). BUDGET
  4a. Unpaid bills.
  4b. Paid bills.
  4c. Invoices.
  4d. Current year's budget.
  4e. Budgets from the past five years.
  4f. Gate receipts.
  4g. Purchase orders.

(5). CLINICS, CAMPS, AND WORKSHOP INFORMATION
(6). DEPARTMENT BULLETINS.
(7). CORRESPONDENCE
(8). ATHLETIC DIRECTORY
  8a. High school coaches; names, addresses, telephone numbers.

8b. College coaches; names, addresses, telephone numbers.

(9). EQUIPMENT AND SUPPLIES
    9a. Catalogs and dealer's price lists and names.
    9b. Uniforms.
    9c. Locks and locker combinations and assignments.
    9d. First aid supplies.
    9e. Event-by-event inventory.

(10). MEET MANAGEMENT
    10a. Past copies of home meet invitationals.
    10b. Current copies of home meet invitationals.
    10c. Past copies of away meet invitationals.
    10d. Current copies of away meet invitationals.
    10e. A "things to do" checklist for administering a home competition.

(11). PRACTICE ORGANIZATION
    11a. Workout schedules, daily by event.
    11b. Workout schedules, yearly by event.
    11c. Previous years' workout schedules by event.

(12). PUBLIC RELATIONS
    12a. Advertising.
    12b. Booster Club.
    12c. Complaints.
    12d. Printed programs from previous meets.
    12e. Mailing lists and telephone numbers.
        12e.-1. Alumni athletes.
        12e.-2. News media—Radio, T.V., Newspaper.
        12e.-3. Other community organizations and contacts.
    12f. Media releases.
    12g. Parent letter, preseason.
    12h. Parent letter, postseason.
    12i. Speeches.
    12j. Team banquet program.
    12k. Team pictures.

(13). POTENTIAL COLLEGE RECRUITS
    13a. Brochures from colleges.
    13b. Letters from coaches.
    13c. Personal friends and phone contacts
        (college).
(14). TRAVEL
    14a. Estimated costs.
    14b. Lodging.
    14c. Maps.
    14d. Transportation.
    14e. Itinerary.
    14f. Ideas.

- Get more from your meetings.
  (1). Before the meeting.
      1a. Write down points to be discussed in proper sequence.
      1b. Set the number of topics realistically to a time limit.
      1c. Give advanced notice of the time, place, and duration of the meeting.
      1d. Prepare and send an advanced agenda.
  (2). During the meeting.
      2a. Start on time.
      2b. Stick to the topics under consideration.
      2c. Keep notes and control the time.
      2d. Note deadlines discussed.
      2e. Set date, times, and place for the next meeting.
      2f. End on time.
  (3). After the meeting.
      3a. Make sure that the minutes are thorough.
      3b. Follow up on any suggestions or recommendations.

- Don't get tied down with paperwork.
  (1). Whenever possible, find another way to communicate, such as the telephone or person to person.

(2). Delegate routine paperwork to your athletic secretary.

(3). Throw away all low-priority files.

(4). Make a book of standardized letters and paragraphs so that correspondence can be easily prepared.

(5). Have incoming mail sorted according to priority.

(6). Act on any correspondence immediately to keep from having to go back and waste time by re-reading.

(7). Dictate correspondence instead of writing it by hand.

(8). Maintain a follow-up file for all correspondence.

3. Organize your practices so that each minute is used effectively and efficiently.

- Before each practice, hold a meeting to make any announcements and outline the workout for the day.
- Jog. This helps stimulate the circulation and other systems of the body. This will warm up the muscles and connective tissues, and aid in eliminating any lactic acid in the body.
- Do flexibility exercises. Stretch each muscle group in static movements to help eliminate injury that ballistic movements cause.
- Develop technique drills. Include all drills related to the overall improvement in running technique. All athletes, regardless of event, need to participate in these drills to improve their overall relaxation and running techniques.
- Plyometric drills should be included. These drills include various hopping exercises to improve overall explosive movement. All athletes need to participate in these drills.
- Do the workout of the day. All workouts for each event must be thoroughly prepared and based on the specific goals you have established.

- Cool down. Do this at the end of each practice session to help slow down the systemic systems and to rid the muscles of lactic acid, which causes stiffness and soreness. A general rule is to cool down until the heart rate is back to normal.
- Begin practice at a specific time each day.

4. You should always have an organizational calendar that outlines a month-by-month, week-by-week, day-by-day program schedule. This will include all goals and objectives you want to accomplish at specific points in the season and will outline your workout schedule from beginning to end.

5. Scheduling is an art in itself. The schedule should be prepared early enough so that your training program can be built around it. It should contain a wide variety of meets from the small duals to the large Invitationals and Championships. You may even want to schedule two meets on the same day so that you can split your team and allow for greater participation. Remember: It is important that all athletes have the opportunity to compete in meets. You cannot expect an individual to train hard all year and never compete. There is something about putting on a school uniform and racing against another team that brings the best out in most individuals. Always judge ability by competitive performances. After all, that's the bottom line in any sport.

6. All trips should be well planned to cover any eventuality. Set up an itinerary that includes:

- the time to report to the bus
- the time the bus will depart
- what equipment to bring along
- where you will be staying and the track you will be competing, including the name, address, and telephone number of each

- the approximate time and where you will be returning

7. All athletes need to have passed a physical examination, have proof of hospitalization insurance and parental permission before participating in your program. Usually the local medical association will administer the physicals if you express the proper appreciation for the donation of their valuable time. If they are unable to help, contact the M.A.S.H. unit of your local National Guard or your Health Department.

8. With the tight budgetary problems facing most high school athletic programs, it is necessary to engage in fund-raising projects to ensure the continued quality and quantity of equipment and facilities.

One of the best and easiest ways to raise money is to have an active Booster Club. This club is usually comprised of parents and interested supporters of your program. With a booster club actively working to help your program, you won't have to worry about having to raise money yourself. Most booster clubs find success in raising funds through membership drives; handling concessions at all athletic contests; selling advertisements for programs; and sponsoring concerts, carnivals, and dances. Unfortunately, a great many booster clubs are active only during football or basketball season and little effort is put into other sports. This leaves you and your team the responsibility of raising money. Successful methods of team fund raising include:

- Car washes.
- Bottle drives.
- Candy sales.
- Dances.
- Magazine sales.
- Jewelry sales.

- Donkey basketball and softball games.
- Celebrity basketball and softball games.
- Raffles.
- Auctions.
- Sale of t-shirts, hats, decals, ribbons, etc.
- School Carnivals.
- Special community project work days.

9. Keep accurate and detailed inventory and expense request records. These records should include a list of, and the condition of, all uniforms and equipment, the estimated needs and expenditures for the upcoming season, and all expenditures and receipts from the last five years. This is necessary to justify your needs and expenses for the upcoming year. If you have a self-sustaining or money-making program, you will have the leverage necessary to deal with your athletic director and principal in using athletic funds for all your needs.

ORGANIZATION OF STAFF AND FACILITIES

How you use your staff and the condition of your facilities as they affect your daily program will greatly enhance the feelings of security and loyalty of your assistant coaches and your team.

1. The number and positioning of assistant coaches will determine where you position yourself during practice to adequately coach and supervise each event. If there is just yourself or one other assistant, you must plan your schedule very carefully to work with each event throughout the week. Sometimes, if you plan the physical layout of the track accordingly, it will allow you to work with more than one event at the same time.

2. Set up the workout schedule on a hard-easy basis. It is impossible for any athlete to work hard every day. The body cannot endure the stress of such a schedule. On days

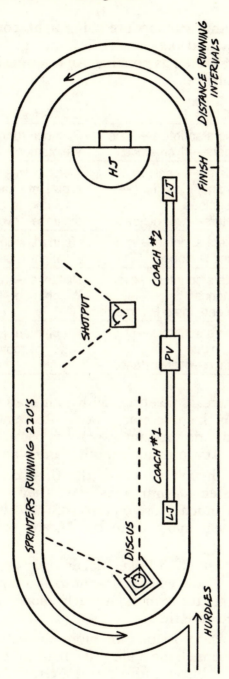

Diagram 2-1

that the distance runners are going light, concentrate on another event, and vice-versa. It is important to work with each athlete as often as possible. An example of a workout schedule might be:

	COACH # 1	COACH #2
MON.	Hurdlers-sprinters—Pace Jumpers—Plyometrics	Distance runners—Pace Weightmen—weight room

TUES.	Hurdlers—Technique
	Long and Triple jump—
	   Technique
	Sprinters—over distance
		Weightmen—technique
		High jump and polevault—
		   technique
		distance—over distance

WED.	Hurdlers-sprinters—speed Distance—speed	Jumpers-weightmen— weight room
THURS.	Hurdlers-sprinters—over distance Long and Triple-Plyometrics	Distance—over distance Weightmen—technique

FRI.	Hurdlers-sprinters—
	   technique
	Distance—over distance
		Weightmen, jumpers—
		   weight room

3. Hold weekly meetings with your staff to plan your workouts for the upcoming week. Remember that all athletes cannot do the same workouts because of varying ability levels. Try to group by ability and plan accordingly.

4. Even though you have the final decision in all workouts, listen to your assistants. They will be much happier and much more enthusiastic and loyal to your program if you make them the "head" coach of their events.

5. Above all, don't linger, delay, or waste time during the workout. Know what you want to accomplish, accomplish it, and get the team home early enough to study and enjoy some leisure time.

6. Whenever possible, for more efficient use of your coaching personnel, the male and female programs should be combined. This will afford you several advantages:

- It allows each member of the coaching staff to specialize in an event. This in turn enhances coaching effectiveness.
- It offers consistency of instruction to each athlete.
- Most programs are strong in a specific area because the coach may be knowledgeable in that area. By combining the staff, it allows each athlete to benefit from every coach's specialty.
- Combining both staffs offers better organization, better utilization of facilities, and more effective time management for both programs.
- With both the men and the women training together, combining both staffs will allow a much better coach-athlete teaching ratio.

6. Facilities are a very important part of your program. They are a showcase for your program both for spectators and for prospective athletes. They should always be well groomed and accessible. If the athletic department won't help you with something you want for the track, raise the money and do it yourself. Even if it means mowing the grass, painting the exchange zones, digging the pits, and repairing the hurdles yourself, keep your facility in A-1 condition.

7. Along with outstanding facilities, dress your squad in attractive, high-quality uniforms. A well-groomed, well-dressed team will have a much better self-concept because they feel good about their appearance.

8. Keep updated track and field publications on the reserved list in the school and community library. Also have as many training and technique films as possible accesible for use with your team.

9. Know your rule book. Make sure each athlete knows the general rules in addition to the rules for each specific event.

10. Recruit and educate an officials group to officiate at all home contests. You will be surprised at the number

of volunteers you will get from the faculty and the community. Host several training sessions and socials for your officials group. The more closely they identify with one another, the more efficient and effective their work will be.

RECRUITING—GETTING AND KEEPING THE ATHLETE

In most circumstances, success lies in numbers. Theoretically speaking, the more individuals you have on your team, the more talent you will have to choose from and the more events you will have covered.

As in any school activity, your track and field program is for any interested member of the student body. Anyone who wants to should be allowed on the team as long as they meet the scholastic and physical examination requirements. *Do not cut anyone from the team.* You never know when someone will mature and develop into an outstanding athlete. It may be that scrawny little ninth-grader who will become the 6'3", 180 pound, 9.3 sprinter in two years. Invite every one out and work with everyone. Your primary requirement for participation should be a willingness to become a better athlete.

It is not as hard as you think to recruit an adequate number of prospective athletes for your team. You have to go about it in a systematic and organized manner.

1. Begin with the younger athletes. The only way you can ensure that your program will perpetuate itself is to always have an adequate number of ninth and tenth graders on your squad. If your feeder schools have a track and field program, it makes your task much easier. You can scout their meets and encourage their athletes to continue with your program. Your presence at the meets will let the prospective athletes know that you are interested. Get to know the feeder school coaches and offer to lend your expertise and services when needed because having the coaches on your side is a definite plus.

If the only feeder school program is an intramural program, offer to help officiate at their championship meet. Bring members of your own team, dressed in competitive uniform, to the meet and have them mingle with the participants—encouraging continued involvement in track and field. It is especially valuable to bring those members of your team who were in that feeder school last year. The participants will identify with them.

2. Organize an assembly at your feeder school(s) where you can sell your program to the student body. Bring along several of your outstanding team members to help sell the program. Again, it is especially important to bring along several young, successful, athletes who may have been at the feeder school(s) the year before. From this assembly, establish a list of prospective team members and encourage them to participate in your summer program.

3. When school begins in the fall, have periodic announcements made for all prospective track athletes to come see you. Also touch base with the new students from your feeder school(s) to make sure of their continued interest.

4. Place attractive posters around the school advertising your program. Place articles in the school newspaper, and if possible organize an assembly of the entire student body to sell your program. Once your list of prospective athletes has been established, you will have the foundation from which to expand your team.

5. Contact the physical education instructors in your school. Have them evaluate all of their students and give you a list of those individuals who, in their opinion, might be able to help your program. If possible, have them administer a physical fitness test to all their students. Use the results from this test to begin your recruiting.

6. One of the most effective means of recruitment is to use your own team members. Have them give you the names of students they think can help the program. Offer a

prize for the team member who brings the most students to practice that end up finishing the season out.

7. Go to the coaches of other sports. Sell your program to them and let them know what you can do to help them if they will encourage their athletes to go out for track and field. Encourage the sharing of athletes with all the sports, not just one specific sport.

8. Issue personal invitations to individuals to become members of your program. Often, all it takes is a personal word of encouragement from you to interest a prospective athlete.

9. After all available avenues of recruitment have been exhausted, compile a master list of athletes and have each fill out an information sheet.

10. Now begin running grade checks on everyone, every week. Use this as a means for remaining in contact with each individual during the off-season. Offer words of praise for those who maintain a high academic average and offer help to those who are struggling. Your genuine concern will keep the individual interested and enthused. Remember, if they can't do it in the classroom, they won't have the opportunity to do it on the track.

Once an athlete has come out for the team, keep him involved. In order to do this, each individual must be able to comprehend his self-worth and follow his own progress and development.

1. Set up some kind of permanent individual record system. This can consist of:

- a list of the top-twenty performers, all-time, in each event
- a ranking of each individual's best marks as the season progresses
- a list of how your athletes' performances compare with the best performances in your county, conference, district, region, and state

SEMINOLE HIGH SCHOOL
DEPARTMENT OF ATHLETICS

305/322-4352, Ext. 232
2701 GEORGIA AVENUE
SANFORD, FL 32771

TRACK AND FIELD DATA SHEET

NAME_____ GRADE_____

DATE OF BIRTH_____ TELEPHONE NUMBER_____

PARENT/GUARDIAN NAME_____

ADDRESS_____

DID YOU RUN TRACK LAST YEAR?   YES_____   NO_____

WHAT EVENTS ARE YOU INTERESTED IN COMPETING IN?_____

_____

BEST TIMES AND DISTANCES FROM LAST YEAR_____
****

CLASS SCHEDULE

FIRST SEMESTER_____ SECOND SEMESTER_____

CLASS_____ TEACHER_____ CLASS_____ TEACHER_____

1._____

2._____

3._____

4._____

5._____

6._____

Home of the Fighting Seminoles

• a Hall of Fame list of all past state champions, state place winners, and all-Americans which can be included on a "Who's Who in Track and Field" board displayed in a prominent place in your school

2. Place a school record board and an all-time total-points-scored-in-a-season board in a prominent location in your school. All records should be updated each year.

3. Install a well-lighted trophy case in a prominent location. Display all trophies and plaques along with 8 × 10 color pictures of all state champions, state place winners, and all county, conference, district, region, and state championship teams.

4. Establish a system of awarding letters that takes into consideration all place finishers, not just winners. An example would be to award points towards a letter of equal value to the points scored in a competition.

GRADE	POINTS NEEDED TO LETTER
9	15
10	20
11	25
12	30

DUAL, TRI, AND QUAD MEETS:	Award the points scored by the individual in these meets towards the total points needed for lettering. Divide relay points by four.
MAJOR INVITATIONALS:	Double all points scored and award them to the point totals. Double all relay points and divide by four.
CHAMPIONSHIP MEETS:	Triple all points scored. Divide all relay points by four and then triple for the point total.

If you have an athlete who is the number one performer in an event on your team, that individual should letter regardless of the number of lettering points accumulated throughout the season. In addition to letters, certificates of excellence should be awarded to those individuals who do not miss a day of practice during the season.

5. A team banquet at the end of the season is essential for recognition of team members. It can be a simple buffet affair where each team member is responsible for bringing a covered dish. All parents, school officials, teachers, boosters, and the media should be invited. At this time, each team member should be recognized for his contribution to the season. Letters and certificates of excellence, along with any county, conference, district, region, state, and all-American recognition should be awarded at this time. Special awards given should be:

- High-Point trophy
- Most Valuable in the Field trophy
- Most Valuable on the Track trophy
- Most Valuable to the Team trophy
- Most Improved Performer trophy

These awards should be voted on by team members with you and your assistants having the final decision. Above all, make each team member feel important, wanted, and needed and your team will remain large.

6. Be democratic and fair in your dealings with team members. It is important that the most unskilled individual feel as important as the star on the team and be treated the same in all manners of discipline.

Seniority should have its advantages. Those athletes who have been dedicated and in your program for several years should have special privileges. It is important however, that you notify the remainder of the team why these privileges are being granted and that they too can earn them after a specified length of time.

7. Emphasize fundamentals in your teachings. The foundation must be properly laid for future development. If the athlete feels that what is being taught is proper

technique, he will feel secure and be satisfied with your program.

8. Arrange a variety of competitions that have something for everyone. Everyone should be allowed to compete. The greater the number of students you allow to compete in each meet, the greater the number who will stay in your program. Remember that if a student competes in an activity in which he has a chance to succeed, it will be more valuable than just allowing him to compete for the sake of competition. Individual successes will bring larger numbers to your program and keep them there.

9. Make early workouts easy and fun. A great many newcomers to your program are still unsure if they want to really make the commitment. The longer you can keep them with you, the more committed they will become.

In such a long season the human body cannot sustain nor can the mind endure hard work day after day. Workouts should be fun and progressive in nature, allowing each person to develop at a steady rate as the season progresses.

10. Once trials begin early in the season, see that no one is consistently winning or losing within a given group. Establish workout groups based on ability. You cannot expect a ninth grader to train on the same level as a senior. This will only destroy the younger athlete's confidence and interest.

11. Publicize the athlete's accomplishments both in the news media and at school. There is nothing more rewarding to an athlete than hearing his name over the P.A. in the morning at school or reading it in the newspaper.

12. Provide incentives for team members throughout the season. As they become more competitive and their performances begin to reach school record, county, conference, district, region, state, and National standards, they should be rewarded and recognized.

- For outstanding individuals, their names can be placed on their jerseys. The jersey will be worn from year to year and kept after graduation.

- Regular T-shirts, in school colors, bearing the team name and logo may be awarded. This is a status symbol that identifies the wearer as a select member of the team.

- Competition spikes can be awarded to all returning county, conference, district, region, and state champions.

- Award jackets to all members of county, conference, district, region, and state championship teams.

13. Make a concentrated effort to secure college scholarships for your outstanding seniors. This will help underclassmen to realize the importance of good grades and hard work. It will also show them that you care about their futures.

SELECTING THE RIGHT EVENT

Placing the right person in the right event can make all the difference in the success or failure of your season; having a happy, hard working, and content team; keeping a large number of athletes interested and involved in your program; and having properly organized and efficient practice sessions.

There is nothing more disorganized or frustrating for an individual than not knowing what event to be training for each day.

- Urge every person to try various events during pre-season and early in the season.

- Begin practice early enough so that you will have time to experiment.

- In distance running, pole vaulting, and hurdling, psychological factors are almost equal in their significance to the physical factors and require careful consideration.

• Body type and structure can give an indication about proper placement, but the best test of ability in a specific event is actually performing that event. This should be done under actual competitive conditions.

Until such decisions can be made, there are several tests that can be used to identify general athletic potential.

Jumping Events

The most important qualities in the jumper are speed and inherent spring or jumping ability. Speed is measured during a 40-yard dash from a standing start. Ideally, anything under 5.0 and the individual has good speed. Of course, the faster the better.

The vertical jump is the best indicator of jumping ability. In this test, the athlete attempts to see how high his center of gravity can be raised during a standing jump. This will determine the degree of explosiveness he has.

VERTICAL JUMP SCALE

OUTSTANDING	30″ and above
EXCELLENT	26″-29″
GOOD	23″-25″
AVERAGE	20″-22″
FAIR	17″-19″

You will also find that the individuals who run the 40-yard dash the fastest and have the best vertical jumps will also be your best sprinters.

In the pole vault, look for 40-yard dash speed and general gymnastic ability.

Throwing Events

In the throws, a quick arm is essential. Size and bulk can be added through a weight training system, but if the student does not have the quick arm, his development will be limited. The best indicator of the quick arm is the kneeling basketball throw.

SCALE FOR KNEELING BASKETBALL THROW

EXCELLENT ---90' and over
GOOD --75'-85'
FAIR --60'-74'

Sprints

In most instances, sprinters are the backbone of the team. Great teams are separated from good teams by one or two individuals with the ability to make up a large deficit and win the race. The sprinter can be used anywhere from the 880 on down.

The following exercise is the most effective way to measure an athlete's ability to run fast.

1. After warming up, have your athlete perform a 40-yard acceleration sprint, gradually building up to full speed.

2. Time the athlete for 60 feet after reaching full speed.

3. With this information, you can compute velocity.

$$\text{VELOCITY} = \frac{\text{Distance run}}{\text{Time}}$$

4. If the male sprinter can sprint over 40 feet/second and the female over 36 feet/second, you have an excellent sprint prospect.

40 yards maximum speed	60 feet-timed
	Coach

PROFILE OF A SPRINTER

1. Actual body height: _____
2. Predicted stride length: Height × 1.17 plus 4" or
   leg length × 2.11
3. Actual stride length: $\dfrac{\text{Distance}}{\text{Number of strides}}$

4. Stride Frequency: $\dfrac{\text{Number of strides}}{\text{Time}}$

5. Velocity at maximum speed: $\dfrac{\text{Distance run}}{\text{Time}}$

Hurdles

The 40-yard dash and the vertical jump can be used to help screen potential hurdlers. The distance covered in five bounds from a standing start will give an indication of both leg strength and power.

SCALE FOR STANDING FIVE BOUNDS

EXCELLENT---42'-42'6"
GOOD ---40'-41'-11"
FAIR --38'-39'11"

An intermediate hurdler should be able to cover 330 yards over eight hurdles. The person who can sprint 330 yards without hurdles in under 40 seconds is a definite prospect. If that individual also uses a left leg lead leg, the chances of being successful are very high.

Middle and Distance

Go to the physical education classes and administer an 880-yard run.

1. Have the class lie down and relax for five minutes. Take their pulse at the beginning and end of this period.

2. Have the class run the 880 all out for time. Look for a 2:30 or better.

3. At the end of the 880, immediately record all pulse rates and record them. Take the pulse every minute after this for five minutes. The quicker the pulse rate drops back to normal, the better conditioned the athlete.

4. Let the class rest for fifteen minutes and then run them in another 880 for time. Again record the pulse rates.

Ideally, those individuals with two fast 880 times of equal speed and a pulse rate that drops back toward normal quickly will be your best candidates.

THE OFF-SEASON PROGRAM

Other than intramural programs, most communities do not have middle school or junior high school athletics. If this is the case in your community, don't be concerned. You can develop your own talent through a community program offered during the summer months.

The primary benefit of a summer program is not so much the talent that can be nurtured as the local interest that is created in the sport. Parents will come out to watch their children compete, find out that the sport is exciting and interesting, and will continue to follow your program during its season. With more community interest, your program will attract a larger turnout.

These summer competitions should be well organized but very low key. All events should be held in each age group, with awards given to everyone who competes. These awards can be solicited from local businesses. No entry fee should be charged for the competitors. All meets should be held one day a week, in the evenings.

It should not be mandatory for all your returning athletes to attend these meets, but it should be strongly suggested. At the end of the summer, you can host an All-comers Championship, and give out medals or some other nice awards. It makes a great end-of-the-year get-together. Recruit your coaching staff and parent volunteers to officiate.

TIME SCHEDULE

6:00 pm--Field Events (three efforts)
7:00 p.m. --Running Events

AGE GROUPS AND EVENTS

6 and Under	7-8	9-10	11-12	13-14
Long jump	Long jump	Long jump	Long jump	Long jump
40-yard dash	60-yard dash	100-yard dash	Triple jump	High jump
	100-yard dash	220-yard dash	High jump	Pole vault
		440-yard dash	100	Triple jump
			220	Shotput
			440	Discus
			880	100
			mile	220
			60 low hurdles	440
				880
				mile
				60 low hurdles
				440 relay
				mile relay

Age groups 15-16, 17-18, and 19-29 will compete in the same events as the 15-16 age group. Additional age groups above the age of 30 may be added if the participation warrants it.

Get your athletes involved in the TAC Junior Olympic program if they are interested. It can be a great motivational factor when they realize that they can qualify all the way to the National Championships.

I have found through experience that the summer should be a fun time for students. Young people need a break from the daily grind of hard work, just as we need a break. By requiring your team to train in the summer, you are defeating the purpose of your summer program. Let them know when the meets are, when the weight room will be open, when you will be available for help. Encourage them to train by all means, but *do not* require it. Allow them to enter the events they wish to compete in during your summer meets. You will find that more of your team will train and compete in the summer if you leave it to them. Let them enjoy themselves.

After school begins in the fall, any of your athletes who are not out for another sport should become involved in a sound, systematic flexibility and weight program. It is not necessary that they do a great deal of running at this time. However, the strength and flexibility they gain from this will carry over into track season. It is also a good time for your motivated jumpers, sprinters, and hurdlers to develop their power by using plyometrics.

You may choose to be demanding and require this of your athletes. Again, it goes back to your philosophy. If the athlete is properly motivated and can see the value of hard work and self-sacrifice in the scheme of becoming successful, you will not have to demand. If the athlete has not reached this point in commitment, any work performed will be half-hearted and totally unsatisfactory.

The primary goal of your off-season and summer programs is to keep the athletes active, enthused and interested in track and field. Any positive psychological or physical gain from this is a definite plus for your program.

Organization and management are a necessity for an effective program. Without it, the members of your team will be unsure of what is going to happen next. They must feel wanted and secure if they are to function up to their capabilities. You are responsible for this.

3

Public Relations and Promotion— The Key to Community Support

PUBLIC RELATIONS AND PROMOTION DEFINED

If you hope to produce teams that are perennial contenders for league or state championships, you must realize that coaching is more than just training young athletes to be physically and psychologically prepared. You also have a responsibility to help your athletes and your program receive recognition from the student body, administration, faculty, and community. This recognition will show each athlete that his dedication and sacrifices are appreciated and will help the general public to experience, learn, and appreciate the same values the athletes appreciate. This recognition is communicated through the art of public relations and promotion.

Public relations is a way to give the public information that will build goodwill and prestige, and foster a friendly attitude toward your program.

Promotion or advertising is an introduction to a product (in this case your team) that attempts to arouse curiosity, and interest, by promising a service that can be of benefit to the public.

Your main task in this area is to find a way to disseminate information about your program to the public in a positive, creative, and attention-commanding manner. If your program is perceived as positive and worthwhile, it will receive support.

ADMINISTRATION

It is extremely important that you remember that the promotion of varsity athletics must be maintained at a level that is secondary to the intellectual and social service aspects of school life. No matter how important you feel track and field is, it is an extracurricular activity and a direct extension of the educational process. The responsibility for administering your program rests with the school administration, not with outside groups.

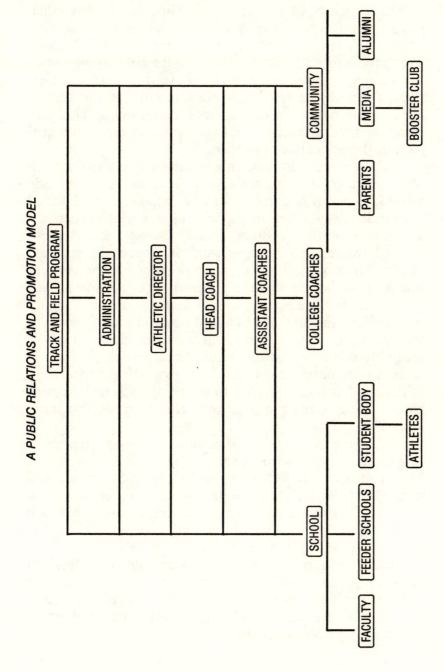

A PUBLIC RELATIONS AND PROMOTION MODEL

Your principal is the bottom line in the organizational, promotional, and public relations scheme of your program. Without positive support from your principal, your program will never develop to its fullest potential.

Inform the administration of your program objectives. These objectives should contain positive and definable educational goals as well as athletic goals. This will show the administration that your program is an integral part of the educational process.

Advise your principal on a regular basis of the accomplishments of your team. This should not only include athletic accomplishments but also academic and social accomplishments. Let the principal know who has become a member of the National Honor Society, is being recruited by various colleges, and is improving scholastically. There is nothing more important for the general image of a school, and your program, than to have an All-American who is also a National Merit Scholar.

Be flexible and learn to adapt to the changing needs of your principal. Throughout your coaching career, you will probably work for more than just one principal. Each is different in basic ideas and understanding concerning athletics. You must be able to adapt to each new administrator, sell your program, and still maintain the same level of excellence.

Your involvement in and commitment to such organizations as coaches associations, civic groups, and church organizations will indirectly reflect on your school and administration. The more involved you become as a positive influence in these organizations, the more positive publicity your school will receive. Make your principal proud that he has you on his staff.

Make it a point to notify your principal well in advance of any meetings you may be attending and the purpose for those meetings. Also inform him of any offices you have been elected to or awards you have received so that he can publicize them.

Ask your principal to present the end-of-the-year awards at the team banquet. If you are dedicating any of these awards in the name of a specific individual, organization, or business, have your principal handle the public relations aspect with the community. If any of your athletes receive college scholarships, have their pictures taken for the local press with their parents, the principal, and yourself.

Encourage your principal to attend meets, help officiate at home meets, or present awards at your major invitationals.

Establishing a good rapport with the administration is critical. Often the administration becomes involved in programs only when something negative has happened. Invite them to become a part of the positive aspects of your program.

A teacher, a coach, a school's entire educational and athletic program is only as effective and viable as the administration will allow it to be.

ATHLETIC DIRECTOR

Your athletic director is the individual to whom you are directly responsible. He is the individual who will approve requisitions, conduct meetings concerning all aspects of the total athletic program, and is directly responsible to the principal for the entire athletic program.

Being an athletic director means being constantly under the gun. The details are endless, the pressures intense, and the problems constant. It is essential that you operate your program in such a professional manner that the A.D. can rely on you to ease some of his burden.

You should take care of the eligibility, prepare your own competitive schedule, secure your own officials for home meets, take care of all the arrangements necessary to operate a home competition, prepare your own facility, and take care of any and all travel arrangements.

Once your A.D. has developed confidence in your ability to handle the normal, everyday administrative details of your program and relieve him of those duties, he will be much more willing to cooperate with you.

You will find it easier to justify the wants and needs of your program if you have an excellent working relationship with your athletic director. This can only be brought about through your sincere and honest effort to promote the integrity of your program.

HEAD COACH

As head coach, you are directly responsible for everything that occurs within your program. You are the chief spokesperson and the number one public relations and promotions person. How you conduct yourself, how you interact with others, and the image you project will do more to help or harm your program than any other factor.

This all relates back to your philosophy of life, education, and athletics. You can be overbearing in your promotion and alienate people or you can work with others and build a firm foundation for the future. Ultimately, your greatest public relations tool will be the satisfaction of the individuals associated with your program. The way you conduct yourself will determine this satisfaction.

ASSISTANT COACHES

If you, as head coach, delegate responsibilities to subordinates and they fail to carry them out, you are responsible. You will receive the credit for a successful program and you will receive the criticism if your program fails. It is important for you to choose your assistants very carefully and work with them to develop those attributes you feel will lead to success in your program.

It is your responsibility to delegate the amount and type of responsibility and authority you feel your assistants are competent enough to handle. It is also your responsibility to see that they conduct themselves in a way that will bring credit to your program. Any actions or comments that they make will indirectly reflect on you as their superior.

Allow them to come to you with any and all questions and concerns. Listen to and make an honest effort to answer all of these concerns. The people who are in a position of leadership in your program must be content or their dissatisfaction will eventually erode the confidence of your athletes.

As head coach, you must constantly work with your assistants. Lay the guidelines down for them to work within, and allow them the responsibility to be themselves, as long as it affects your program in a positive manner.

FACULTY AND STAFF

The faculty and staff at your school are as indispensible as the key members of your team. Remember: If an athlete can't perform in the classroom, he will not have the opportunity to perform on the track.

You should establish a rapport with the members of the faculty. Present yourself to them as a professional who is concerned not only about a student's athletic progress but also his academic and social development. This may be accomplished by informing the faculty about your program, its goals, and its objectives.

Encourage faculty participation in your program. The best way to accomplish this is to circulate a memo at the beginning of each season asking for volunteers to help officiate at home competitions. Stress to the faculty that if students see them actively participating in after school activities, they will see them as normal human beings, interested in total student development. In most cases, this will help eliminate discipline problems in their classrooms and the members of your team will see that those faculty members are interested. You will be pleasantly surprised by the number of volunteers you will get.

Another excellent way to establish a rapport between the teacher and athlete is to supply each faculty member with a weekly newsletter updating them on the accomplishments of your athletes. There is nothing more gratifying to the athlete than to have a teacher congratulate him on his new personal record.

Express your gratitude to those faculty members who do help at your competitions, at the end of the season with a nice thank you card, an invitation to your awards banquet, and a small gift.

This support is a two-way street. The classroom teacher has a very difficult job in education today. Mounting criticism of the teaching profession and a seeming lack of interest on the part of many students and parents have eroded much of the positive support that they receive. Anything that you can do to give them positive support is definitely in the best interests of your program. This should include encouraging the athletes to finish their work, hand it in on time and maintain self-discipline in the classroom. This support can play a positive leadership role in class discipline. If you have an athlete who is having a problem in a specific class, you should support the teacher and reinforce any disciplinary or academic measures he takes.

If possible, provide before or after school study halls for those athletes who are having academic problems and make an attempt to use as little school time as possible for competitions. This will let the faculty know that you care about each athlete's academic progress.

The English department can encourage reading of track fiction for reporting. The speech department can use track topics for reporting and speech making. The social studies or history department can utilize the history of the Olympic Games for reporting. Fatigue, muscle development, heart recovery time, and warm-up are some of many topics the science department can emphasize. The Mathematics department can assign metric measurement and time and distance problems that relate to track and field. All this can be accomplished if you take the time to organize projects and present them to the department chairpersons in a persuasive manner.

The members of your physical education department are your greatest asset. It is through their efforts that you can identify potential prospects you may have missed otherwise.

FEEDER SCHOOLS

The lifeline of your program are the various feeder schools that send you students each year. Even if they do not have an athletic program at their level, it is imperative that you maintain a positive, ongoing relationship with each contact person at each school.

Send a letter to each contact person and his Principal each year congratulating them on running an excellent program. Secure from them a list of all the prospective track athletes who will be attending your school during the next year. Write each prospective athlete a letter letting him know he has been recommended for your program and encourage him to participate in track and field during the following year. As soon as school begins in the fall, contact him again on a personal basis and encourage his involvement in your program.

Be willing to help the middle schools out whenever possible. Provide clinics and demonstrations for them.

Allow them to use your facility, when it is available, for meets or practices and provide special events for them to run in your invitational track competitions.

STUDENT BODY

If you have laid the proper groundwork for administrative and faculty support, it, along with the athletes' excitement and positive attitude, will filter on down to the student body. Your team's success will give them a rallying point for school pride in the spring.

Take advantage of their support and promote it by holding several pep rallies during the season. Football and basketball have them. Why not track and field? Rallies create enthusiasm and offer immediate and positive feedback to team members if they are well organized. Use cheerleaders and the band. Introduce team members to the student body and have them give a few simple demonstrations on the mechanics of starting, hurdling, long jumping, and so on. You may want to give a brief presentation on some of the general rules that govern track and field and how you keep score at meets, to give them a greater understanding of and appreciation for the sport. Films of your team in action or even Olympic champions could be shown to help promote awareness.

Another excellent way to create student awareness is to stage a competition during the school day and have the student body released to watch it. When inviting a team for this kind of meet, pick a nearby school with whom you have an active rivalry. Limiting the number of entries to two per event, and one event for each person, will allow greater athlete participation and move the meet on more quickly. Don't keep score. Introduce the contestants in front of the stands before each race and by their field events area before the event begins. As the meet progresses, your announcer can supply information and keep everyone informed of performances.

Ask the various school service clubs to get involved in your home competitions by serving as hurdle crew members, recorders, and finish line personnel, or by working with the field events. They may also want to sponsor certain events at your major invitational.

The more you can encourage your student body to become involved in your program, the greater your chances of picking up new team members for next season.

ATHLETES

A major portion of the public relations process is establishing a strong relationship with your athletes. Once you have accomplished this, your program will perpetuate itself with your athletes doing the majority of your public relations for you.

One principle remains true when dealing with others. We all enjoy, crave, and thrive on positive recognition. Public relations then becomes a matter of providing positive recognition for your athletes. This can be accomplished in a variety of ways.

BULLETIN BOARDS: Your school must be track conscious. Everywhere the students and faculty go, they must be made aware of some phase of the track and field program. The school bulletin board can be utilized with timely articles, features, and pictures, all on some phase of track. This material should be kept up-to-date and colorful. The location of these boards should be where the entire school will come into contact with them.

RECORD BOARD: A track record board placed where students, athletes, and even the community can constantly see it is of great value. List the school records, the state and National records as well. This can become a great incentive to the athlete as well as a spark in developing a sense of pride in members of the school and community. If a record is broken, take the old one down and give the plaque to the individual who held it.

In addition to the school record board, place an 8 × 10 picture of all state champions in a highly visible area in the school. This will assure immortality for the champion and is something he can show his own children over the years.

LIBRARY: Contact your librarian and arrange to have a separate section of the library devoted to track and field. Help the librarian stock it with good fiction books as well as books and films on technique. Current periodicals such as *Track Technique* and *Track and Field News* should be included.

TRACK PUBLICATIONS: You and your athletes can develop a press booklet and hand it out at the beginning of each season. If you put it together properly, this booklet will explain and promote your program. The booklet can include:

- a letter to the athlete welcoming him to the team, encouraging him to work hard and see the season through, and emphasizing what his participation will do for the program
- the schedule for the current season
- the goals and objectives you have established for the upcoming season
- all school, county, conference, district, regional, state and National records
- the result of all meets from the previous year, including copies of the newspaper clippings on these meets if possible
- last years' Top 15 Performances from your entire state
- specific team rules
- past state champions and state place-winners
- all places and performances from major post-season competitions such as the Orlando Sentinel Golden South Track Classic, the Golden West, the Interna-

tional Prep Invitational, and the Junior National TAC Championships
- a list of all of your nationally ranked performers
- a list of all of your track and field All-Americans
- a Hall of Fame that requires the athlete to be an All-American, state champion, state place-winner, or Nationally ranked in order to become a member
- a list of your top ten single season high point scorers
- a list of the top 10 or 15 all-time performances and or performers in each event
- a page for each athlete's personal goals for the coming season
- various motivational phrases and articles that you may have run across as space fillers and additional pages
- a roster of the team with a sketch about each person for the upcoming season
- facts about the school
  - location
  - historical information
  - principal
  - enrollment
  - conference
  - school colors and nickname
- information about the coaching staff
- an attractive cover

It is important for the self-image of the team that they be outfitted with attractive uniforms and warm-up suits. It is also important for team members to project a positive image by behaving correctly and being well groomed.

As a coach, you should become involved with your athletes. Keep abreast of student activities and personal accomplishments. Do not be afraid to ask team members their opinions on various matters and let them have input in some decisions.

Personally meet and speak with each athlete as often as possible. Make them realize that they are Very Important People where you are concerned.

Send each team member a letter during the summer just to let them know you are still thinking of them and are looking forward to the coming school year.

COMMUNITY

Community may be defined as anyone who comes into contact with your program but is not directly associated with it. This includes businesses, organizations, and the public in general.

In order to build a firm foundation of public support, you should take advantage of every opportunity to present a program or speech at civic or community organizations. You may use a slide or movie presentation, bring your outstanding athletes, present progress reports as your season progresses, or speak on athletics and academics in general. Let these important community leaders see that the school has employed a competent and dynamic individual who is capable of conducting an exemplary program.

Ask local businesses to sponsor awards for your invitationals or a track-athlete-of-the-week award. They can display these awards in their business windows. Also ask them to display pictures of team members, competitive schedules, and posters of upcoming events associated with your program.

Distribute your yearly track brochure to all local businesses and industries describing the goals and objectives of your program. Encourage business and civic leaders to attend your competitions and participate in them in some capacity. If they are too busy, ask them to sponsor and print your competition schedule each year to be handed out around the school and community. The Armed Service is an excellent organization for soliciting such favors.

You may have competent individuals within your community who would enjoy serving as volunteer coaches. Encourage their participation, and utilize them as an integral part of your program.

You may be fortunate enough to coach an outstanding individual who is invited to a major postseason competition. In most instances, it is your responsibility to raise the funds needed to send the athlete. If you have laid the public relations groundwork correctly, you will be able to secure resources from the community to meet these expenses.

Your community is your greatest resource and base of power. If the community sees a need for something that the school is reluctant to grant, they can apply an enormous amount of pressure to help satisfy this need.

PARENTS

You must work very hard to secure the support and confidence of your athletes' parents. They are the ones who are going to allow their children to stay after school for practice when they could be working. They are the ones who are going to make sure their children are up and ready to leave for those early Saturday morning meets. They are the ones who are going to get out of bed to pick their children up after those late Friday night meets. They are the ones who are going to pay for the practice shoes and the competition shoes.

The better a relationship you can build and maintain with the parents, the easier your job will become.

Send a letter to the parents at the beginning of the season letting them know how much you appreciate their cooperation in allowing their child to participate in your program. Also inform them that they will have to make some sacrifices and commitments if their child is to remain on the team. Explain your goals and objectives and tell them that you hope to expose their child to the values of commitment, hard work, loyalty, and self-sacrifice. Ask for their understanding and support in this endeavor. It would be a good idea to enclose one of your track brochures with this letter.

Another letter should be sent at the end of the season thanking them for their cooperation and support and explaining how enjoyable it was working with their child. Emphasize that you are looking forward to working with them in the future. Enclose a summary of your season with meet results and individual performances.

These letters should be personalized and not in some copied form. Let each parent know that he is special.

It is also an excellent idea to send a newsletter home periodically during the season with up-to-date meet performances and a paragraph on each team member and how he is progressing.

Hold an informal meeting with the parents of your prospective athletes prior to the start of the season. Use this occasion to reaffirm your policies and goals. Explain to them how they can best help and encourage their children's athletic endeavors. You might also want to encourage them to join and play an active role in the athletic booster club or even form their own club.

You will always have those parents who feel their child is not being used in the most advantageous position on your team. As long as you are fair to each individual and allow him the opportunity to better himself, you will have very few problems.

Remember to keep the lines of communication open at all times with the parents.

MEDIA

Obtain as much media coverage as possible for your team. There are very few rewards in track and field. One of them is the excitement and personal satisfaction of seeing one's name printed in the newspaper or hearing one's name on the radio or television. It's an excellent motivator for your athletes to know that they are receiving recognition for all the long and hard hours of work.

Of course, it is a much easier task to work with the media in an area where there are only a few schools than in a large metropolitan area where there are many.

You can help yourself by providing the media with important information about your team.

1. Develop a media release schedule for the season. Establish specific dates on which to release information.

2. Send your track brochure so that it can be used as their authority on your program for the upcoming season.

3. Give them unique and special information in the form of workable ideas for stories, rather than vague generalities.

4. Help them to compile a county, conference, or area honor roll to be published on a weekly basis.

5. Provide action photos for use in stories.

6. Invite them to cover your home meets, travel to away competitions, and attend your awards banquet.

7. Be sure to report all meet results factually and in plenty of time to meet deadlines.

8. Send in all material relating to track and field. Often sports departments are looking for material to use as fillers. Why shouldn't it be track and field.

9. Keep them informed about your former track stars and what they are doing in college now.

10. If you have a local cable station, advertise your major meets on it and look into the feasibility of showing your meets.

11. Meet with each reporter and drop by his office for informal visits.

12. Invite them to private luncheon meetings and to Conference or league meetings.

13. Develop an "All Opponents" team and have it published. Send a copy of the article to the coach of each athlete for possible publication in their newspaper.

14. At the end of the season, write each reporter and his superior a special thank you letter letting them know what an outstanding job they did of covering your season.

Anything you can do to promote positive public awareness of your program through the news media should be done. It will add to the prestige and the integrity of your program.

ALUMNI

Your alumni can be very beneficial in helping to perpetuate your program. Encourage them to continue their support by becoming actively involved in it. They may want to help officiate at meets, become volunteer coaches, or just contribute in any way possible to the continuation of your program.

You may want to schedule an Alumni-Varsity competition where they will have the opportunity to come back and compete against your present and future stars. If you stay at one school long enough, you may be coaching the children of your former athletes. It will make your job much easier if you stay on good terms and kept them actively involved in your program.

BOOSTER CLUB

The majority of high schools have semiactive booster clubs. By semiactive, I mean that during football and basketball season they are very active and then their interest wanes. Work with the booster club and encourage the parents of your athletes to join. Encourage them to run for office and assume an active leadership role in the club.

Meet with the board of directors and outline the needs of your program and what they can do to help you meet these needs. Your greatest asset in dealing with the booster club is having a program that is successful, has a large amount of participation, and has parents that are active in the booster club. If you can show them that your program is viable, they will work with you.

In some circumstances, individual sports have their own booster clubs. If this is the case, you must work very hard with all the parents to develop an active interest and to find avenues for helping your program. If you can solicit sponsors for your team, do it. It takes money to run a program and the more financially independent you are of school funds, the better off you will be.

COLLEGE COACHES

Maintaining contact with college coaches is an effective way to help your superior athletes to receive scholarships each year.

Develop a card system of all the coaches you come into contact with. Call them periodically and send them a list of your outstanding athletes, in addition to any others in your area who might be prospects. Invite the coaches to your meets and send them the results of all the major meets or outstanding performances you happen to run across.

The best public relations device to use with them is to always be honest in your evaluation of prospective recruits. If you feel that someone very talented in athletics, but has moral, behavior, or academic problems, let the coach know. Don't recommend all of your athletes highly when you know that several of them are not suited for higher education. If the college coach wants to take a chance on someone, let him. If you maintain your honesty and integrity at all times, they will keep coming back.

If you live close to a university, volunteer to help officiate at their home competitions. Offer to help them run track or cross country camps or loan them your vaulting or high jump pits for their camps.

Public relations and promotions are tools that will enhance your program. They can turn a good program into an excellent program and can help to perpetuate parental, student, and community interest in a sometimes less-than-glamorous sport. Develop your own interest, and turn your program into a local and financial success.

4

Developing a Sound, Systematic Training Philosophy

The development of a training program is one of the most important and difficult tasks for any coach. It is important because it is the guide for the individual workouts that will develop the athlete, and it is difficult because it must constantly change to meet the changing needs of the athlete.

When you have a well-planned training program and execute it efficiently, the athlete will have greater respect and more faith in you as a coach.

All training programs involve phases where there is emphasis on some particular aspect of training. Within each period, the individual workouts are arranged in cycles so that there is a day of rest between cycles. Each cycle usually builds on the preceding one. The critical factor in the success of any program is the arrangement of workouts, cycles, and phases so that they are meeting the individual needs of the athlete, and are improving the weakest aspect of performance at that particular time.

PHYSIOLOGICAL BASIS FOR TRAINING

Physiologists have identified three sources of energy that cause muscular contractions. In each case, the last step in the reaction involves the breakdown of adenosine triphosphate (ATP) to produce energy and adenosine diphosphate (ADP).

Of these three energy sources, two of them are termed as anaerobic or "without oxygen." These occur with reserves that are present in the body and can be sustained for only short periods of time.

When there is a need for energy, the first reaction will provide it for 10 to 15 seconds of muscular contractions. This muscular reaction involves the combination of ADP and Phosphocreatin (PC) to produce ATP. The second reaction can respond for 30 to 40 seconds and involves the combination of glycogen and ADP to produce ATP and lactic acid. This lactic acid is converted back to glycogen in the liver, which supplies fresh glycogen. The conversion process is slow and isn't of much help in races of 3 to 8 minutes in duration.

The third energy source is termed as aerobic in nature or "with oxygen." It is a source of energy available for several hours of mild exercise where the body is functioning at its "steady state." This involves the combination of glycogen, free fatty acids, ADP, and oxygen to produce water, carbon dioxide, and ATP. This can continue as long as the ingredients are available in the body.

Training of the anerobic energy sources consists of working at a high intensity over a short period of time. The pulse rate will rise to between 170-200 beats per minute. Lactic acid will accumulate in the blood, the athlete will be out of breath, and if he does not slow down, the muscles will stop working until this oxygen debt has been repayed.

In aerobic training, work loads consist of relatively low intensity over periods of long duration (20 minutes to several hours). The pulse rate has to rise to between 120 and 170 beats per minute in order for a "training effect" to occur.

The benefits of aerobic training include:

- greater muscular endurance
- increased lung capacity
- increased blood supply to the muscles
- larger, more supple blood vessels
- an increase in the number of vessels to and around the muscles
- reduction in the percentage of body fat
- an increase in the stroke volume in the heart

All of these factors result in a greater ability to move oxygen from the lungs to the muscles, where it is used in muscular contractions.

Some of these results are also achieved through anaerobic training. However, too much high intensity training can increase the chances of overtraining and lead to injury. It is necessary to temper and mix the correct amounts of aerobic and anaerobic training to achieve the maximum training effect.

PRINCIPLES FOR PLANNING A TRAINING PROGRAM

There are three main categories in training:

- physiological
- psychological
- tactical

We will cover the psychological and tactical aspects in later chapters.

PHYSIOLOGICAL PRINCIPLES

1. The body adapts to stress through the improvement of the functioning of the major systems.

2. Training must place stress on all three energy systems to improve their efficiency.

3. The degree of stress (workload) should gradually increase as the athlete improves.

4. Training must be designed to prepare the athlete for the type of performance that is the goal.

5. Anaerobic training should follow long and careful preparation by aerobic training.

6. The program should include training for strength, speed, endurance, flexibility, and power. The proportions of each varies with the different phases of the program.

7. Cycles are used so that there is variation in workloads over a specified period of time. This does not

necessarily mean a 7-day work cycle. Many training programs today use 10- to 15-day cycles.

8. The total demands on the individual (training, school, job, social life) must be in equilibrium with the recovery processes (eating, sleeping, rest, recreation).

COMPONENTS OF FITNESS

Endurance

There are two forms of endurance: strength endurance and circulatory-respiratory endurance.

Strength endurance is the capacity of the muscular system to perform movement against a resistance force. This is demonstrated through the use of many repetitions. Circulatory-respiratory endurance is the capacity of the capillary beds in the muscles and lungs to hold oxygen and it reflects the body's ability to resist fatigue. This type of endurance is developed through aerobic exercise which conditions the heart and blood vessels so that a larger circulatory-respiratory function can develop.

Basic overall endurance can be developed in several ways.

1. *MARATHON TRAINING:* This is volume training that consists of slow, continuous running at a relatively low speed over distances of up to 30 miles. The heart rate will approach 150 beats per minute. Because of the nature of this type of training, it offers little stimulus to the development of muscle strength in the legs, nor does it greatly stimulate the heart. It is, however, the best method for improving the capillary system.

2. *FARTLEK:* Fartlek or "speed play" originated in Sweden and is one of the most misused methods of training in the United States. It is characterized by a long run, over undulating terrain, which is broken into a series of slow jogs and fast sprints, interlaced with a series of rhythmic gymnastics.

Fartlek courses should include long hills—up to 500 yards if possible—where the runner can attack them.

This system of training has for the athlete many advantages if used properly.

- It develops a sense of independence in the athlete.
- It is physically challenging, but mentally relaxing because the athlete is away from the track with no set distance measured off to run.
- The softer running surfaces of woods and fields take strain off the body.
- You can practice this anywhere and at any time.
- It is the natural way to run—to run until you tire and then to back off and recover, and then to run again.

Its major disadvantage is that it is hard for immature and inexperienced athletes to adjust to the freedom of speed play. They often misuse it for its name and play at it.

3. *INTERVAL TRAINING:* Dr. Woldemar Gerschler has been credited with this method of training. It is basically pace work controlled by the pulse rate and coach over a set distance or distances that never exceeds 400 meters. The classic interval training distance is 200 meters.

The key to interval training is the pulse rate during the recovery period. It should be raised to over 160 beats per minute during exercise. The recovery period is a minimum of 30 seconds and a maximum of 90 seconds. During this time, the pulse rate should drop back to 120 beats per minute or under so that the capillaries can begin to close down. At this time, the next repetition is run to again stretch the heart.

If the heart rate has not recovered to 120 beats or less after the 90-second rest interval, the workout has been too severe or too long and should cease at that point for re-evaluation.

An easy formula to remember for developing interval training sessions is:

D—The *Distance* to be run

I—The *Interval* or rest between each repetition

R—The number of *Repetitions* to be run at each distance

T—The *Time* or pace for each repetition

The workout can be manipulated by adjusting the formula in the following manner.

- Increasing or decreasing the distance
- Decreasing or increasing the rest interval
- Increasing or decreasing the number of repetitions
- Increasing or decreasing the time

A good interval workout should cover two to three times the actual racing distance in any one workout.

The advantage of interval training is that it improves the ability of the heart to increase the volume of blood it pumps in a much shorter time. Another advantage is that the athlete can train at his race pace. The major disadvantage is that it is basically anaerobic and stressful.

The easiest method for monitoring the heart rate recovery time is to have the athlete find the carotid artery in the neck and place any finger except the index finger on it immediately after running. Once the pulse has been found, say "go" and start your watch. The athlete begins counting heartbeats. At the end of 6 seconds, say "stop." The athlete then multiplies the number of beats by 10 to obtain the heartbeats per minute.

The sooner the heart rate drops back to normal during the recovery period, the better conditioned the athlete is.

4. *REPETITION TRAINING:* This is often confused with interval training. They are not the same. In repetition training an athlete runs a given distance at a predetermined speed a certain number of times with *complete* recovery between repetitions. Repetition training is usu-

ally run over up to three-quarters of the racing distance at race pace or faster.

5. *HILL TRAINING:* Hill training has been termed as "speed work in disguise." This may be the best high intensity exercise for the development of anaerobic fitness. Soviet research indicates that repeat hill training up a 10 percent grade has produced heart rates of up to 200 beats per minute. Normally heart rates of this nature are only produced in maximal speed sprinting on the flat.

Both uphill and downhill running should be utilized. Uphill for strength and downhill for speed. In the downhill running, grades of no more than two or three degrees should be used. If the grade is any steeper, the pull of gravity will be too strong and the athlete will not be able to maintain correct body posture.

Downhills should always be run before the uphills because it is a speed workout and the athlete needs to be fresh. All hill workouts should be completed by running as many repetitions on the flat as on the hills to balance the muscular strain on the legs.

The distances run may vary from 400–600 meters for the distance runners to 40–80 quality meters for the sprinters. Speed should increase up to 10 percent after eight weeks of training.

Speed

All of us have heard the old adage that "sprinters are born and not made." This is true to some extent, because each individual is born with a certain number of white muscle fibers (fast twitch) as opposed to red muscle fibers (slow twitch).

The white fibers have a limited blood supply, produce rapid and powerful contractions, fatigue easily, and are designed for speed. The red fibers are approximately three times slower than the white, have a greater blood supply, do not fatigue as easily, and are best suited for endurance.

It would be ridiculous to attempt to take an individual with a more red fibers than white fibers and turn him into a sprinter. It is possible, however, to improve that individual's speed to its maximum potential.

In track and field, we are concerned with horizontal speed. This is made up of two components—leg speed and stride length. Improvement in either will increase speed as long as one is not improved at the expense of the other.

Leg speed or the rate of striding is governed largely by the individual's physiological make-up. In every individual, there is very little room for improvement, with the exception of modifying his basic running technique to better utilize speed. Stride length may be improved by:

- better utilization of sprinting technique
- increased stride length as a result of increased leg strength
- increased flexibility

If an individual can lengthen his stride while maintaining the same rate of leg speed, horizontal speed will increase.

In addition to increasing stride length, improvement in speed can come through an improvement in the level of maximum speed endurance, acceleration ability, and reaction time.

Reaction time can only be improved by exercises that require sudden changes in body position or that are begun on a given signal (such as starts). Acceleration can be improved by exercises demanding a change from a complete stand still to maximum speed.

A general set of rules to follow in using workouts for the development of speed is as follows.

1. Speed can be developed by sprints of three to five seconds in duration. This will improve the speed of the muscles and nerve impulses of the central nervous system, which need to be programmed for high intensity speed.

2. All repetitions should be performed at maximum speed with complete recovery intervals.

3. No repetition should exceed the actual racing distance.

4. Varied speed training should be used to break speed plateaus.

5. It takes between five and six seconds to reach maximum speed. Generally, one cannot accelerate after sixty meters if sprinting all-out. It is the individual who maintains relaxation and technique, and slows down the least over the last forty meters who wins the race.

6. Once maximum speed is reached, it may be held for a period of twenty to fifty meters, depending upon the individual's level of development.

7. Approximately eighteen percent of a sprinter's total effort is expended on pushing air aside. This is why faster sprint times are recorded at high altitudes and with trailing winds. There is less air to push aside.

Notes on Horizontal Speed

1. Leg speed × stride length = horizontal speed.

2. Leg speed should range from 4½ to 5 strides per second.

$$\text{Stride Frequency} = \frac{\text{Number of strides}}{\text{Time}}$$

3. Stride length should range from 7 to 8½ feet.

$$\text{Stride length} = \frac{\text{Distance}}{\text{Number of strides}}$$

4. Maximum stride length may be approximated by multiplying the athlete's height by 1.17 plus 4 inches for the male and by 1.2-1.3 for the female or by taking the athlete's leg length and multiplying it by 2.11.

A Method for Measuring Speed

1. After warming up, have your athlete perform a forty-meter acceleration sprint, gradually building to full speed.

2. Time the athlete for sixty meters after he has reached full speed.

3. With this information you can compute velocity.

$$\text{Velocity} = \frac{\text{Distance run}}{\text{Time}}$$

4. If your male sprinter can sprint over forty feet per second and your female sprinter over thirty-six feet per second, you have an excellent prospect.

Strength

High school athletes are running faster, throwing farther, and jumping longer and higher than ever before. The good, natural athlete can no longer dominate. It is the good, natural, strength-trained athlete who is dominating the national scene today.

When an athlete reaches a peak, it is the limit of his strength that has been reached. With increased strength, new and higher levels of performance can be achieved.

In 1948, research by Dr. Thomas DeLorme found three basic guidelines to follow when developing a strength training program.

- Strength is developed through high resistance with low repetitions.
- Endurance is developed through low resistance and high repetitions.
- One method cannot substitute for the other.

There are several other physiological principles to be kept in mind when using strength training.

1. In order for a muscle or a group of muscles to increase their strength, the muscle must be overloaded, beyond its normal strength. As the muscle adapts to this overload, it must be further overloaded.

2. Specificity is very important. In order to achieve maximum transfer of training, the same movements relative to a specific skill should be performed through its entire range of motion.

3. Muscle fibers grow larger with increased strength but the number of fibers remains the same. If a muscle is torn or pulled, new muscle fibers do not grow. Connective tissue grows into these voids.

4. Strength, endurance, flexibility, and power increase through regular overloading of the muslces involved.

5. Weights should be lifted in a slow, continuous movement so that all of the nerve impulses can reach the entire muscle group at one time. This maximum muscular tension causes the muscle to go through a fast, forceful contraction. An increase in the speed of lifting will decrease the muscle's ability to produce high tension. If the resistance remains constant, however, an increase in the speed of lift will contribute to muscular power.

6. Capillarization is increased, which makes glycogen and nutrients more available to the fibers for energy, and allows more expedient elimination of waste products from the muscle. This will delay the onset of fatigue and make oxygen more accessible to the fibers.

7. Muscle protein will increase and muscle fat will decrease.

8. For maximum strength development, one should train at 70 percent to 80 percent of his maximum strength.

9. In order for a program to be beneficial, it must be regular. For example, an athlete should train three times per week in the preparatory and skill phases and two times per week during the competitive phase.

10. The rate of strength gain will slow as maximum strength potential is approached.

11. Both the red and white muscle fiber groups should be exercised.

12. Best results will come from four to five sets of five to six repetitions. As weight increases, repetitions decrease.

Strength training is a must for your program. Without it, your athletes will never develop their true potential.

Power

Explosive power is defined as the ability of a stationary body to propel itself into rapid movement. Explosiveness must be specifically developed in the joints and muscles involved in the actual event in order for the body to be propelled from a stationary position to maximum movement in the least amount of time.

Previously, it was thought that the only way to develop power was through strength training. However, the strongest person in the world isn't necessarily the most powerful. To bridge this gap between strength and power, plyometric exercises were introduced by the eastern Europeans.

The concept of plyometrics is based on the following physiological premises.

1. The faster a muscle is forced to lengthen, the greater the tension it exerts.

2. The rate of stretch is more important than the magnitude of stretch.

3. The farther a muscle is prestretched from its natural length before contraction occurs, the greater the load it will be capable of lifting.

4. A concentric contraction (shortening) is much stronger if it immediately follows an eccentric contraction (lengthening) of the same muscle. This is termed as the myotatic or stretch reflex.

In essence, the muscle resists overstretching by causing the stretch reflex, which produces a powerful contraction in the same muscle. An example of this can be seen in jumping events. In order to jump higher, one must first bend at the knees (eccentric) before exploding upwards (concentric) in the opposite direction.

The best method for converting yielding energy to overcoming energy as quickly as possible is through the use of depth jumping from specific heights. This involves dropping from a predetermined height and, immediately upon landing, rebounding upwards. These exercises may be performed in one of three ways.

1. Straight jumping where the athlete begins from a predetermined height, jumps straight down, and explodes back into the air as quickly as possible off one or both feet.

2. Jumping from one box at a predetermined height down onto the ground and then exploding back up to another box at a predetermined height.

3. Performing a series of movements or a complete skill from a predetermined height. An example would be hopping off a box, completing a series of hops, hopping on and off another box and executing another series of hops.

For ultimate effectiveness, one must jump from a predetermined height of 2'5½" for maximum speed and 3'7¼" for maximum, dynamic strength. Any height other than the maximum or minimum will be ineffective in power development. Also, any overloading of the athlete's own body weight will destroy the effectiveness of depth jumping. *SPEED* of movement is of the utmost importance.

For the experienced and well-prepared athlete, depth jumping may be performed twice per week with no more than forty repetitions per session. The inexperienced athlete should only depth jump one session per week with twenty to thirty repetitions until a broad training base can be developed. It is recommended that an athlete not attempt depth jumping until his leg strength is at least double his body weight.

These exercises should be performed in sets of ten repetitions with some form of active rest between sets, for example, ten depth jumps, followed by ten fifty meter strides. Because of the severity of depth jumping, sufficient time must be allowed between each session to allow the body to adapt to the stress. They should be discontinued at least 14 days before competition to aid in recovery.

Other forms of plyometrics include any combination of multiple hops or steps on a resilient surface. These too must be performed with maximum effort on each repetition.

Remember: The theory behind plyometrics is to explode as quickly as possible and as strongly as possible on each repetition.

Flexibility

Flexibility is defined as the range of motion a joint or series of joints can move through. This, more than any other factor, limits the performance level of an athlete. The greater the flexibility, the better the performance and the less chance there is for injury.

There are two forms of flexibility. Static or the maximum degree of flexion or extension, and dynamic or the flexibility of motion. Static flexibility involves slowly locking the joint for a period of time and slowly stretching the muscles and connective tissues to their greatest possible length. This reduces the danger of exceeding the extensibility limits of the muscles while also relieving muscle soreness.

The bouncy, jerky movements produced by ballistic exercises cause one set of muscles to actively contract while the antagonistic muscles are trying to stop the contraction. The force generated through this process overextends the extensibility limitations and contributes to muscular soreness and strains.

It is very important for each muscle group to be stretched through a full range of motion in order for it to respond when called upon in a competitive situation.

Dynamic flexibility or elasticity (muscle extensibility) and plasticity (ability of the joint to change or modify its direction) of the joints and muscles determines the amount of torque (a force that causes an object to rotate) needed to move a joint through its complete range of motion at various speeds. This is very important because if the elasticity or plasticity of a muscle is limited, then its ability to generate torque will also be limited. Muscle injuries often occur when the athlete generates more torque than the elasticity or plasticity of the muscles and joints will allow.

Even though very little research has been completed on dynamic flexibility, it is safe to say that the most effective way to improve it is to perform exercises that actually involve the muscles and joints of the event. These flexibility exercises should be performed before the training session begins and after it is completed.

Skill

Skill is the learned ability to bring about predetermined results with maximum certainty and minimum expenditure of time or energy or both.

There are many variables involved in acquiring a skill. These variables, and several theories, will be discussed in Chapter 5. What is important here is that a skill cannot be satisfactorily learned until a certain level of overall fitness is reached. Correct technique can only be practiced until fatigue sets in. The better conditioned the athlete is, the longer he can perform a skill before the onset of fatigue.

All of these fitness components are interrelated in each track and field event. In order to become successful, the athlete's training program must include each component at the desired period in the training cycle. An excellent point to keep in mind when developing this program is that endurance, flexibility, and strength must come before power, speed, and skill can be developed.

ADAPTATION TO PHYSICAL STRESS

The goal of a training program is to develop the stamina necessary to sustain a high rate of speed over the racing distance, free from injury. This stamina is developed by increasing the body's "steady state" (the body's ability to move at a high rate of speed until its energy supplies are exhausted). Steady state is improved through the body's gradual adaptation to stress.

- The body's adaptation to stress will occur within its range of adaptability.
- It will be specific to the stress applied.
- All adaptation occurs during the recovery period.
- If the stress is too severe or too frequent, it will have a negative effect on the body's ability to adapt.

This range of adaptability is called the comfort zone. All work performed outside the comfort zone is either too hard or too easy, depending on whether you're working at the upper or lower levels of the zone. As the body adapts to the stress in the upper levels of the zone, the steady state will improve and the boundaries of the zone will be expanded. Continued stress at the upper levels of the comfort zone will gradually wear the athlete's resistance down and lead to injury or mental staleness. Training sessions need to be planned for lighter, easier days in the lower level of the zone to allow the body to recover and have time to adapt to a previous upper level workout.

FOUR SEASONS OF TRAINING

1. *PREPARATORY:* This is where the foundation is laid for the remainder of the season. The training load will be the greatest with concentration on hard, physical conditioning. Very little skill is emphasized. Endurance, flexibility, and strength are of the utmost importance.

2. *SKILL:* Workloads reach their peak and intensity is increased during this period. A large amount of technique work is done with emphasis placed on preparing for upcoming competitions. During this period, competitions

should be thought of as developmental and used only to evaluate the athlete's progress. How one performs place- or time-wise is of little consequence. Endurance, strength, and flexibility are still emphasized with the addition of speed, power, and skill.

3. *COMPETITIVE:* The intensity of speed loads is increased with longer recovery before and after competitions. This is the championship meet portion of your schedule. The intense workloads are performed at the beginning of the week and are tapered as the competition nears. Flexibility is still stressed, with a cutback in the amount of endurance and strength workouts. Skill and power have been tapered back to minimal levels, while speed is at its maximal training stage.

The individual must be fully rested going into each competition.

4. *ACTIVE REST:* This immediately follows the competitive season. After being under great mental and physical stress during the championship season, the athlete needs to relax, rest, and recover while still maintaining a level of fitness. This is the time to participate in other sports and generally enjoy training at a leisurely rate.

On the high school level, this training pattern can be broken down into six week cycles. Prepare for six weeks, develop skill for six, and compete intensely for six. Participation in another sport is an excellent way to fill the active rest period.

Not all athletes will respond the same to a training program. Your young, inexperienced athletes may need a longer preparatory cycle than the more experienced athletes. You will have to adjust each individual's program accordingly.

TRAINING THEORY

Combining and manipulating all the various factors into a yearly training program is a delicate task. Each event or group of similar events has different requirements for success. These requirements should be evaluated and the program developed around them.

MIDDLE-DISTANCE AND DISTANCE TRAINING

A rule of thumb is that the longer the distance, the more aerobic the training and the shorter the distance, the more anaerobic the training. In middle-distance and distance running sixty percent of the program will be in the endurance area, thirty percent in race readiness, and ten percent in speed work.

The endurance area will utilize all those areas mentioned in the endurance section of this chapter. Race readiness utilizes those areas that will develop the pace, tempo, and tactical aspects of racing. Speed development will come through the use of short, very intense sprints. All of these areas can be worked comfortably into a twenty-one day training cycle.

OVER-DISTANCE: 10-12 sessions.
REPETITIONS: 4-6 sessions.
FARTLEK: 3-4 sessions.
INTERVAL: 1-2 sessions.
COMPETITIONS: 0-3
REST: is worked into the over-distance at a leisurely pace.
SPEED: 1 session.

The 800- and 1,500-meter individual will receive more speed work than the 5,000- or 10,000-meter person and may even occasionally move down with the 400-meter runners for workouts.

SPRINTING AND HURDLING

These areas are related, with hurdling receiving more technique days until the skill has been perfected. Then the hurdler becomes basically a sprinter.

In sprinting, we are speaking of the multi-sprinter. The individual who is trained as a 400-meter runner and then is either moved down to the 100 and 200 or moved up to the 800. It is important that your sprinters be trained in this direction to better utilize their talents.

Sprint and hurdles workouts consist of strength, power, speed endurance, tempo endurance, endurance, strength endurance, speed, and technique. Strength training is composed of traditional weight lifting. Power will include plyometrics. Speed endurance training includes workouts of high oxygen debt and lactic acid build-up. The total workout distance is determined by multiplying the race distance by 2.5. Repetitions and distances will range from 10×100 meters to 2×600 meters with almost complete recovery between each. Tempo endurance is done at slower speeds with less recovery time, stressing rhythm, tempo, and correct sprinting biomechanics. Endurance training is purely aerobic and improves oxygen uptake and recovery time. Strength endurance consists of hill training and resistance running. Speed is composed of workouts of maximum intensity with full recovery time to ensure quality.

A sprint training cycle can be broken down into an eighteen-day cycle. The following are the recommended training sessions per cycle. The cycle is repeated for the desired time period until it is time to move into the next cycle.

	Preparatory	Skill	Competitive
Endurance	4	2	1
Tempo Endurance	3	3	2
Strength Endurance	4	3	1
Strength	6	6	6
Power	4	6	3
Speed Endurance	3	3	5
Speed	2	4	6
Rest	2	2	2
Competition			2

FIELD EVENTS

The field events can be broken down into three areas of concentration:
1. long jump.
2. all other jumps.
3. throwing events.

The long jumper is predominantly a sprinter or hurdler. The majority of the practice time should be spent doing the sprint workout. Only one session per week is spent on actual long jumping.

All other jumpers will spend more time on strength, power, and technique, as will the throwers.

	Preparatory		Skill		Competitive	
	Jumpers	Throwers	Jumpers	Throwers	Jumpers	Throwers
Endurance	4	4	2	2	1	1
Strength	6	6	6	6	6	6
Power	5	5	6	6	3	3
Speed	2	2	5	2	6	2
Technique	1	1	5	5	4	4
Strength Endurance	4	4	2	2	1	1
Speed Endurance	3	—	2	—	1	—
Rest	2	2	2	2	2	2
Competition	—	—	2	2	2	2

This chart is based upon an eighteen-day training cycle

Flexibility is an automatic part of the warm-up and cool-down everyday, for all events.

Developing a training program can be very complex but also very easy if the basic physiological principles are followed and blended with the needs of the athletes. They must show continuity and progression towards peaking for the championship competitions at the end of the season.

5

Learning a Skill— The Coach Makes All the Difference

A coach may be well versed in the technical elements of track and field, but without the ability to transmit this knowledge so that each individual understands and follows directions, that coach will never become successful.

In track and field, the aim is to develop a pattern of movement designed to achieve maximum performance for each individual. This pattern should be learned so well that it becomes a part of the athlete. Any deviation from this basic pattern should feel wrong.

Even though individuals learn skills in various ways, there are certain, specific laws for learning that are common to all.

LAW OF EXERCISE

The more frequently a stimulus and response are associated with each other, the more likely that particular response will follow that stimulus. Practicing a skill the correct way each time will mean that in most cases the correct response will be achieved in competition.

LAW OF FREQUENCY

An athlete must repeat a skill frequently to learn it. Frequent practice sessions over a period of time are important. However, there is a law of diminishing returns associated with this concept. An individual can only practice a skill correctly so many times before the onset of fatigue. If the skill is practiced after this, learning will become slowed and improper. The training session then becomes a failure. This makes it extremely important to develop a base of physiological stamina before beginning skill practice. Also, skills should be worked on at the beginning of the training session, when the athlete is fresh.

LAW OF RECENCY

Movements practiced recently are more easily remembered. This implies that athletes should review key points of their events:

- before a training session begins
- before competition
- at the end of a training session

Practice can either be physical or mental. If physical, exercises should be selected that simulate the actual movements of the skill. Mental imagery is also important in order for the individual to actually think through the correct technique.

LAW OF FORGETTING

During rest periods, the body forgets undesirable movements, and mental imagery sometimes results in a sudden improvement following this rest. This is extremely important when an athlete has reached a plateau and is making no further progress. A short rest period may help to breach this plateau. An athlete can rest for too long, however, and will soon forget correct movements. Rest periods should be of moderate length and include some form of activity to maintain general stamina.

LAW OF EFFECT

This involves the principle of reinforcement. Learning is much more likely to take place if it is accompanied by a feeling of satisfaction. You must positively reinforce those techniques that are desirable and discourage those that are not. An individual will be much more likely to improve if he knows that it will earn him a reward. This may be either tangible—acceptance or an improved perform-ance—or intangible—a general feeling of satisfaction.

LAW OF COMPETITION

The majority of athletes who have trained properly will improve their performances by competing. More opportunity must be provided, however. Far too often we schedule competitions that have limited entries or that are of such caliber that only the most highly skilled can be successful. Additional meets need to be provided so that the beginners can have more opportunities to compete. This could include junior varsity meets, splitting the team for alternate meets on the same day, or conducting compe-titions with unlimited entries.

THE LEARNING CURVE

Physical skills cannot be learned without attempting them and few can be acquired in a single trial. If perform-ance could be measured in some way and plotted on a graph against the amount of practice, it would show the individual's learning curve. This curve varies from person to person and activity to activity. It is affected by certain variables.

1. There may be a period during which no measurable learning occurs.

2. There may be a period during which gains between later trials are greater than the gains between earlier ones. This curve of increasing gains is seen with a beginner or someone attempting a complex skill.

3. A curve of decreasing gains may be found when an athlete is working at the secondary level or is an average performer who wishes to become an expert. This is the opposite of the increasing gains curve.

When an athlete begins to learn a new skill, his learning curve has an increasing gains pattern, but as the learner moves closer to the goal the pattern changes to decreasing gains. This curve will level off at the goal of perfection or at the physiological limits of the individual. It is virtually impossible to reach perfection in a skill and individuals reach their limits of flexibility, strength, speed, endurance, and power, before their physiological potential has been reached.

When an individual does reach a level where no improvement is shown with further repetitions, it is called a plateau. This is a period during which there is no definite change in performance, even though the individual continues to practice. If the athlete continues his effort long enough or takes a short rest he can pass this period of stagnation with a sudden burst of ability that carries him to a much higher level of achievement. However, some athletes may become so discouraged that they will give up altogether. It is advantageous to avoid plateaus if at all possible.

When an individual begins to learn a new skill he frequently begins with a tremendous amount of enthusiasm and interest. At the same time, he may find that past experiences similar to the skill can be an advantage to learning the easier parts of the present skill. Progress is evident and very rapid. Gradually this rate of improvement slows down and the individual becomes discouraged, loses interest, and wants to quit.

A plateau can also occur if the learner has acquired bad habits during his training that prevent further progress. These habits must be eliminated. Eliminating bad habits frequently results in a lowering of performance for a time. Many athletes are not willing to accept this setback period and therefore limit their improvement permanently.

A plateau may also arise when an athlete has reached the attainable limit possible through a particular learning method. You can avoid this by teaching good form and correct technique from the beginning. This gives the athlete fundamentals and style that create a basis for future development.

Plateaus do occur during training. Each athlete must realize and accept this. If they are approached from a positive standpoint, such as "I have to reach a plateau before the next level of improvement will come," and if correct coaching techniques are used from the beginning, the effects of a plateau will not be drastic and the athlete will soon move on to higher levels of performance.

FACTORS AFFECTING THE ACQUISITION OF SKILL

The conditions that determine the speed with which your athletes can reach a given level of performance may be divided into:

- those that vary with the skill and the methods of learning.
- those that vary with the individual learner.

INSTRUCTION

If left alone, the learner usually practices the first method that brought him some success. However, it may not be the correct method. The old argument that says people will learn from their mistakes and find the best way is not usually true. The learner without instruction tends to continue with the method that was first learned. Once this becomes a habit, it is extremely difficult to change. Sheer repetition alone will not result in improvement. Training, where one is required to use reason and intelligence and has a coach to receive instruction from, is the best means for rapid improvement.

Proper instruction will increase the flexibility of behavior and will prevent the learner from falling into a set pattern of incorrect techniques.

The way in which an athlete performs a task the first time will largely determine the way he subsequently performs it. It is best to begin the correct way and not just allow the athlete to experiment on his own. It is very difficult to retrain a bad habit. Even if you think it has been corrected, it may reappear under the extreme pressure of competition. The learner should be encouraged to vary his actions until he hits upon some pattern of movements with good form. Those are the ones to be emphasized.

What works for one individual may or may not work for another. An excellent key to remember is the more meaningful the skill is to the learner, the easier it is to learn, and the fewer mistakes he is likely to make.

VISUAL INSTRUCTION

The most common form of visual instruction is demonstration. Your demonstrations should be of excellent quality to specifically show the desired action.

If you feel you cannot adequately demonstrate a skill and have no other athlete to draw on, a film of an expert performing in competition can be used. It should be shown at natural speed so that the beginner can get the feel of the action. The demonstration should be brief and no analysis should be attempted. The action should be immediately attempted with occasional looks back at the model for reinforcement. The sole purpose of the demonstration in the early stages of development is to give the athlete an idea of the skill being attempted so that he can develop a feel or kinesthetic sense of it.

After the initial stage of learning, more attention can be given to detail to increase the learner's understanding.

This can be done by slowing the film down and analyzing each specific movement or drawing attention to fundamental requirements for success.

MANUAL OR MECHANICAL INSTRUCTION

This involves actively pushing the individual's body through the desired movements or providing artificial support so that the technique can be carried out. This is not the most desirable of aids because the kinesthetic sensations the learner feels will be different from those he feels when performing on his own.

There are several occasions when this technique might be beneficial:

- when the learner seems incapable of copying the desired movement
- when the complete action cannot be completed because of some minor difficulty
- when the skill is a dangerous one

VERBAL DIRECTIONS

These are not necessarily beneficial. It depends on how and why they are given. If they are overdone with beginners, the athletes have trouble understanding them. If you describe movements relatively accurately by using technical terms, it may take a long time, create feelings of uncertainty, frustration, or boredom, and impede learning.

In the early stages of learning, verbal instructions should be brief and used mainly to direct observation. Detailed explanations should be kept to a minimum. As the learner progresses, more detailed verbal directions and analysis of movement can help in increasing the meaningfulness of the skill and giving new insights into it.

This will provide reasons for particular movements, and help the individual to learn to correct his own actions.

Ultimately each individual must perform without your help. Therefore, after the skill has been learned, your instruction should be interspersed with longer periods of silence. Otherwise, the athlete may become too dependent on you. Your instruction must take the form of building on the interests, abilities, and temperament of each individual rather than having a model of what should be in your mind and making the individual adapt to that model. Your goal should be to help each individual develop his own individuality. This is very important because learning is done by the learner and is not accomplished by some kind of transmission process from you.

KNOWLEDGE OF RESULTS

If a person practices without knowing the results of his actions, his improvement in performance will be very slow. Feedback on each performance will allow the athlete to choose what is good in a performance and incorporate it into subsequent practice.

The learner should be given specific information as soon as possible. If you have good observation powers you can provide immediate feedback at critical times. With a large team and a small staff, this becomes very difficult unless you are well organized. One method for alleviating this problem is to set up exercises where precise information can be obtained by the individual with limited feedback from you. This is extremely practical for the more experienced athlete. You become an advisor who helps to analyze and isolate situations that the athlete can practice on his own. This will leave you with more time to spend with beginners. An occasional offering of praise once or twice during a practice is enough to keep the experienced athlete working hard and happy.

Try not to impose too specific a technique. Watch for the correct movements and build on them. Each individual is different and will not fit into a mold of how you would like them to look. They will progress faster if you stress their good points. Do this with praise and encouragement. Stressing the bad points is only beneficial when you wish to break down bad habits. This helps to create learner dissatisfaction and a quest for positive reinforcement.

Often too much criticism can lead to overcorrecting and cause more problems. This is especially true with an athlete who wants to do everything right, and, therefore, mentally freezes and can't do anything. The important factor is to give more positive reinforcement than negative, and place the individual in situations where he will achieve some success.

MOTIVATION

The most important factor in the acquisition of skill is motivation. Little improvement is made if the learner is not interested or doesn't care about what he is doing. No amount of repetition or time spent in practice can change this. The quality of practice is important. When the learner sees value in the work he is performing and when he enjoys it and looks forward to it, your job becomes easier.

Here are some helpful hints for creating a more motivational environment.

1. First impressions are important when introducing an activity. Make it fun and easy. Get the athlete hooked on it.

2. Make sure the athlete experiences success in each training session. It will keep him coming back for more.

3. Public praise is helpful if not over used.

4. Punishment should be used sparingly and only in extreme cases. It only serves to frustrate the athlete. Pretty soon he becomes more concerned about the punishment than the activity. It is no fun going to practice when he knows that there will be a punishment for every mistake.

5. Competition can lead to improved performances. It is also a test of present skill level and helps to alleviate the boredom of repetitive activities. An athlete can also compete against himself by engaging in activities that test him and compare his present results with previous workouts.

Anything you can do to provide incentive and variety in your training sessions will be of infinite value in your quest for improved performances.

DISTRIBUTION OF PRACTICE

Gross motor skills require a short time period for practice because of the need to warm up both physically and mentally. This minimal time depends on the nature of the skill and the warmup requirements of the individual.

There is also a limit to the usefulness of any practice period. This limit depends on the motivation of the learner and the amount of fatigue encountered. This does not necessarily imply physical fatigue. Psychological fatigue can be expressed in subjective feelings of tiredness, boredom, or in an increase in the number of errors and periods of inattention. It is useless to continue practicing a skill when this occurs.

The length of practice is determined by the physical ability and motivation of each learner. Many experienced athletes will set up a workout and go through it at all costs. This is acceptable for building strength and stamina. For the development of skill, however, as soon as the athlete loses motivation and begins to make consistent errors, that portion of the workout should cease before he forms bad habits or injures himself.

For the development of skill learning, a short period of intense effort and attention is better than a half-hearted longer period. In the beginning frequent periods of short length are advisable. After the foundations have been laid, practices can become longer. In general, they must be long enough to enable the athlete to get warmed up and should cease when fatigue or a loss of interest begins to introduce errors; when good responses are beginning to break up; or when bad habits are being formed. You may use short rest periods and introduce new challenges to delay the onset of physical and mental fatigue.

SPEED AND ACCURACY

Because speed is vital to performance, it is a part of the technique and should be emphasized from the beginning. A slow movement is performed differently from a fast one even though the path of movement is not changed. Techniques that require speed and are developed with speed will more easily transfer to performances that require both speed and accuracy. This does not imply that you cannot slow an action down. With the beginner it is important to begin slowly. The speed used however, should be fast enough for the movements to be useful to the athlete. As skill is developed, the speed can increase.

RETENTION

The more an individual practices a skill, the easier it becomes to perform. He will also be less likely to forget it, and will relearn it more easily if he does forget it.

TRANSFER OF LEARNING

Learning a new skill can be speeded up, hindered, or changed by previous instruction, or it may not be affected at all. Often in the beginning stages of learning, an old skill will cause temporary interference but still enable the athlete to acquire the new skill in a shorter period of time than would otherwise have been possible.

Transfer is more likely to occur from relatively difficult skills to relatively easy skills and not vice versa. You cannot deal with complex skills by practicing easy ones at slow speeds. Transfer can also occur by learning how to learn. This gives the student a better mental perception of the principles involved in the skill.

VARIABLES IN INDIVIDUAL LEARNING

A student's individual characteristics affect the speed with which he reaches a given level of performance by influencing the rate of learning as well as ability. Ability is influenced by age, inherited characteristics, and previous experience.

AGE

Physiological age, not chronological age, determines when an individual is ready to learn. This maturation cannot be controlled by external forces. It is developed through the natural processes of the body. Strength, motor coordination, reaction time, speed, precision, steadiness, and psychological stability all increase with maturity.

The preschool child engages in exploratory and imaginative play, oblivious to others. Even in the first few years of school, a child's interest is with his own actions. From ages 7 to 11 personal motor coordination is developed. At about age 11, competition and team games become important. Later the individual specializes in certain games and individual sports. In general, the period from age 5 to the beginning of adolescence should be spent on a great variety of personal skills and techniques. Early adolescence can be spent on team games with specialization and individual selection taking place in later adolescence.

Age has an affect on the rate of learning and the individual's ability to comprehend directions. These will improve with age.

SEX

Females mature at an earlier age than males, which has a general effect on learning a skill. Females will be able to learn at an earlier age than males will.

Certain physiological differences have been found between the male and female that affect ultimate performance. However, as more females are training at higher levels, the gap between these differences in certain areas is closing. This might mean that the differences are more social and cultural than physiological.

Of course, the hormone balance of each person determines to a large extent how far they can progress in such areas as strength development, endurance, power, and speed.

INDIVIDUAL DIFFERENCES

Individuals vary in their innate abilities. These will affect not only their initial ability to learn a skill but also their rate of learning and ultimate capacity. Everyone can develop his ability to the utmost through sound and dilligent training. It's just that some have more to develop than others.

In many instances what looks like an individual's inability to learn is actually his lack of previous experience with that skill. This will have a major effect on his initial learning ability. When this athlete gains experience, you may find that he has more ability than someone with previous experience who picked the skill up more easily.

A THEORY OF LEARNING: WHOLE-PART-WHOLE

In the area of athletics, the whole-part-whole method of teaching has been among the most successful. In this method, the entire skill is performed at natural speed to get the feel of what it should be like. It is then broken down into specific parts through the use of exercises that apply to the entire action. Once this refinement of specific parts has been accomplished, the entire action is performed again, evaluated, and plans for future refinement are made.

It takes a long time to adequately master a skill in this manner. If proper motivational techniques are used to keep the athlete interested, this is the best way to completely develop a skill.

Here are some suggestions for breaking a skill down into the whole-part-whole learning sequence.

1. Show a film or have someone demonstrate the entire skill.

2. Without explaining the skill, have the individual perform it.

3. Film the athlete and compare his technique to that of the expert. Point out likenesses and areas where improvement is needed.

4. Break the skill down into exercises that will develop these areas.

5. Perform the entire skill again. Evaluate it. Plan for future training sessions.

THE COACH AS THE PRIME FORCE IN SKILL DEVELOPMENT

How you present the skill, interact with the athlete, and motivate him makes all the difference in skill development. Developing a skill is very tedious work, especially when curves of decreasing gains are reached. Anyone can set up a training schedule and demand that it be completed. It takes an artist to manipulate, encourage, and motivate the individual to enjoy and demand more from himself in a training session. Every young athlete will become discouraged when he reaches plateaus. You have to be able to help him through these trying times, until the plateau is breached with higher levels of achievement.

It is helpful to avoid certain coaching behavior when dealing with your athletes.

NEGATIVE COACHING STYLES

- *INSULTER:* Always downgrades and demeans the athletes. Never has anything good to say. Always embarrasses.
- *SHOUTER:* Always yells instructions. Never sits down to talk with the athletes as individuals.
- *PUNISHER:* Makes the athletes pay for a poor performance with some type of punishment. Never motivates them to do better, only criticizes.
- *DRILL SERGEANT:* Takes pride in being tough and unrelenting. Believes that constant verbal and physical abuse develops toughness and the will to succeed.
- *TECHNICIAN:* Believes there is only one correct technique in a skill. Demands that everyone develop the same technique.
- *PESSIMIST:* Always saying what can go wrong. Never optimistic or inspiring.
- *BIG SHOT:* Wants his athletes to be dependent upon him. Wants to let everyone know he is the coach.
- *SLOPPY:* Disorganized. Never plans practice, forgets equipment, is late for practice.
- *BOSS:* There is only one way and it's his way. Will not bend or admit mistakes. Doesn't want any questions asked, and won't accept alibis or excuses.

- *MOUTH:* Thinks the more instructions he gives the better he is coaching. Confuses the athletes but enjoys hearing himself talk.

There are also positive coaching styles that you can follow to promote better learning.

POSITIVE COACHING STYLES

- *SUPPORTER:* Empathetic. Always behind the athletes. Believes in them and will help them in any way possible to become successful.
- *LEADER:* Remains calm and relaxed in trying circumstances. Projects an image of stability to the athletes. Criticizes in private and praises in public. Acts as a mirror image of how the athletes should act.
- *BUSY:* Spreads himself around and gives positive attention and support to each athlete at each practice session.
- *COUNSELOR:* Shows a real personal interest in all his athletes. Makes himself available to sit down and talk about all interests, not just athletics.
- *SALESMAN:* Sells concepts, techniques, methods, and the entire program by giving convincing and honest reasons for their value and use.
- *INVISIBLE:* Helps the athlete to become independent and perform with confidence and skill without constantly relying on the coach. Presents ideas in such a way as to make the athlete think he discovered them himself. Runs the team by letting the athletes think they are running it.
- *CHEERLEADER:* Always praising and inspiring the athletes on to higher levels of achievement.
- *PROGRESSIVE:* Realizes that each individual is different and will learn and act differently. Does not demand that a certain technique be copied. Looks for and encourages correct movements and individuality.

- *PRECISE:* Always prepared and on time for a workout. Gets things done efficiently.
- *EDUCATED:* Knows the whys and why nots of technique. Uses only the scientific procedures to develop skills.

There are any number of methods for coaching. You must find the method that fits into your philosophy and personality. No matter which method you do choose, the principles of learning set forth in this chapter are appropriate. If you follow them, your job will be much easier and your chances for success much greater.

6

Motivation— Preparing the Athlete for Competition

Being well versed in the technical aspects of track and field and being able to put them across to the athletes are only part of coaching. Motivating athletes to perform up to their capabilities is by far the most difficult and most important facet of coaching.

All coaches have heard the myth of the "burned out" athlete. The athlete who worked too hard, too soon, and either burned out before the big meet or never improved.

This myth is true to a certain extent. However, an athlete does not become physically burned out because of workouts, but he may become mentally burned out because his coach is unable to properly mold and monitor the psychological aspects of the athlete's training and competition.

This ability to monitor, mold, manage, and motivate the athlete accounts for ninety percent of a person's ability to coach. It separates the great from the not so great.

THE IMPORTANCE OF MOTIVATION FOR THE ATHLETE

Individuals participate in athletics for many and varied reasons. Four of the most common are:

1. They either believe or have been told that they possess the athletic ability.

2. Often an individual is searching for any avenue for success he can find and turns to athletics as the answer.

3. Participation in athletics is a vehicle for peer acceptance in a specific school setting.

4. Parental pressure. Often parents have a strong desire for their children to participate in sports, for many different reasons.

An individual's self-image is the ultimate factor in determining athletic success. Discovering what lies within and then learning how to use that awareness is a major factor in improved athletic performance.

Self-image, or self-esteem, or self-concept, is an individual's picture of himself as a person or an athlete. This picture is formed from everything he has experienced since birth. These experiences include all of an individual's successes and failures, triumphs and humiliations, and his reaction to his acceptance or rejection by those individuals most important to him (parents, coaches, peers, and teachers).

The individual sees himself as the sum total of all that has gone before. These experiences become true in his mind and therefore true in their consequences.

Unfortunately, society shapes individuals and tends to create differences between them, only to reward the norm. By the time a coach comes into contact with a person on the high school level, his negative experiences far outnumber the positive successes, and his emotions and attitudes have already formed.

Emotions are a critical factor in a person's ability to respond to the environment. They are strong reactions and help the body to react physically to various stimuli when the need arises. Emotions are an internal feedback system that tells an individual when something feels either good or bad and whether to seek it or avoid it in the future.

Social scientists have defined seven basic emotions that an individual is capable of feeling.

- joy
- sadness
- anger
- love
- anxiety or fear
- shame
- surprise

Individuals differ in their ability to experience these qualities, just as they differ in strength, speed, endurance, flexibility, and power. The more a person knows his own emotional qualities, the better he can prepare himself to participate in a specific activity.

No matter how hard or how easy it is to experience certain emotions, they are a source of arousal and energy in the individual if shaped correctly.

Undoubtedly, the single most prevalent emotion, and the most difficult to shape to advantage, is anxiety or stress.

Anxiety is a term used to describe a state of mind in which the individual is responding with discomfort to some event that has occurred or is about to occur. This discomfort is over something unsettled and prompts the person to worry about the consequences—either real or imagined.

Common physiological symptoms of stress or anxiety are:

- shortness of breath
- "butterflies" or a tightened stomach
- headaches
- hypertension and an uncontrollable "chatter" in the mind
- nausea
- increased perspiration
- ulcers
- tension in the arms and legs

Excessive anxiety may even lead to frequent injury.

The body responds physiologically to images the mind creates. Just as the body responds with tension and anxiety to a nightmare, it responds negatively if the athlete approaches competition with uncontrollable fear or anxiety. This anxiety can cause counterproductive phys-iological responses, such as tightening up, becoming less flexible and therefore more prone to muscle pulls, or losing concentration, increasing the risk of an accident.

In addition, once the injury occurs, undue anxiety may interfere with the individual's ability to recover quickly.

It is stressful enough just to be injured. Not being able to perform up to expectations while injured or wondering when and if one will be able to compete again, places severe tension on the musculoskeletal system, and may interfere with treatment as muscles need to be relaxed during the healing process.

Causes of extreme anxiety or stress range from phys-ical fear, to fear of embarrassment, to anger or hate, or even to the fear of success. The predominant cause of anxiety, however, is the fear of failure.

It is a combination of both the physiological and psychological responses to anxiety that inhibit an athlete's performance. Anxiety needs to be dealt with. The worst way to handle it is to ignore it.

Confidence, overconfidence, and feeling "psyched up" can help an athlete to deal with anxiety.

If an athlete can build his confidence and develop a positive self-image through successful experiences, he has taken a large step toward controlling anxiety and using it constructively.

Overconfidence can result from too much success. All practices and competitions, while being positive experi-ences must be tempered with the knowledge that no one is infallible and that everyone can be beaten.

Success breeds success. It breeds an enhancement of self-image, and with it, a positive attitude toward sports.

This enhancement of self-image gives the athlete the ability to "psych up" for competition. This certain excited way of feeling before competition creates a sense of eagerness, of feeling strong and full of energy. Once the individual learns to control and channel this emotional energy into physical action the role of a participant becomes the role of a competitor.

SPECIFIC TECHNIQUES FOR CONTROLLING ANXIETY

The key to the release of anxiety is the relaxation of the physiological as well as the psychological restraints on the athlete. The following is a simple but effective program for relieving tension on the field.

1. Place the finger tips along the temple area of the head. Close the eyes and inhale slowly while massaging the temple slowly and gently. Count to six and slowly exhale, continuing to massage.

2. Move the finger tips to a position just above the eyebrows and repeat number 1.

3. Inhale as the jaw is tightened. Hold for the count of three and slowly exhale. Feel the jaw relax and loosen.

4. Close the eyes and slowly rotate the neck clockwise. Stop, and rotate it counterclockwise. Inhale and exhale slowly and evenly.

5. Tighten the shoulders. Bring them up, forward, and down slowly into a relaxed position, in a shoulder shrug type action. Feel the muscles relax. The breathing should be slow and even.

6. Repeat number 5, only this time bring the shoulders up, back, and down slowly.

7. Place the palms of the hands together. Push them against one another as hard as possible for the count of ten. Slowly release and relax.

8. Sit upright with good posture. Take a deep breath and tighten the stomach. Hold for the count of ten and slowly exhale and release in a relaxing manner.

9. Repeat number eight, only now tighten the buttocks.

10. Repeat number eight, only now press the heels of the feet firmly against the ground. Hold for the count of ten and release.

11. Breathe deeply through the nose to the count of three. Slowly exhale.

12. Inhale deeply. Hold this to the count of three and release slowly. When performing the breathing exercises, be sure to breathe from the diaphragm.

Repeat this exercise cycle three times in a slow and relaxing fashion. It is advantageous to perform these exercises while listening to soft, and relaxing music.

PSYCHOLOGICAL CHARACTERISTICS OF THOSE WHO SUCCEED IN ATHLETICS

In order to adequately pinpoint the psychological characteristics of a champion, it is necessary to first recognize the characteristics of those individuals who are not successful but who each coach must deal with.

1. ALIBI IKE: This athlete performs well in practices but very poorly in competition. There is always an excuse for poor performance. This individual has no confidence and has a very poor self-image.

2. MUSCLE GRABBER: This individual always looks good in the preliminary events but is rarely good in the finals. Accompanied by failure is some type of pain or injury; usually psychosomatic. When the heat is on during a race, this individual will either back off or drop out because of an injury.

3. LOSER: The loser climbs into a shell because of imagined worthlessness. There is an overall feeling that no matter how hard he works he will never succeed. This person is usually an introvert who is afraid to speak or act because he might be wrong.

4. CON MAN: This is a likeable individual who, after a couple of weeks of feeling out the coach and the team, begins to coach others and neglects himself.

5. UNCOACHABLE: This athlete has a better way of doing everything. He does not listen to the coach and has very little conscience, is selfish, and has no gratitude for those who are trying to help.

6. ANXIOUS: This individual has very little common sense and attempts to hide it by clowning around or goofing off. The anxious individual usually makes mental errors during competition.

7. HERO: This athlete comes from behind or goes all out in competitions that have very little meaning. When up against others of equal ability, he will make a mistake, tighten up, and fall apart.

8. SUSPICIOUS: The suspicious athlete believes that the coach does not care about the athletes and is there to use them for personal gain.

9. INFANTILE: An immature athlete who pouts. He is very emotional, unstable, and cannot handle tense situations with any degree of calmness.

10. BUM: The most difficult individual to work with is the bum. He takes advantage of others, lies, cheats, steals, and does not repay debts. This athlete is an overall malcontent.

What characteristics then must an athlete possess to become successful in athletics?

- ambition
- aggressiveness
- mental and physical toughness
- competitiveness
- the ability to remain relaxed under pressure
- the discipline to be organized

- intelligence
- the humility to accept coaching

The potential for success lies within each person who chooses to participate in athletics. There is an old saying that says "anyone can become a success. It's just that very few individuals really try."

It is the coach's responsibility to deal with each and every individual in an attempt to turn emotional weaknesses into positive energy sources for success.

THE INDIVIDUAL ATHLETE'S ROLE IN IMPROVING SELF-IMAGE

A coach cannot improve an athlete's self-image without the athlete's help. The athlete must want to change and become a better person.

The athlete can begin with the idea that a permanent change is possible. He must analyze his strengths and weaknesses and accept them as something every human being possesses. He must also take pride in his accomplishments and not come up with alibis for poor performances.

Along with this self-evaluation, the athlete must realize that he should never underestimate himself and should be constantly striving to look at failure as part of the learning process that will eventually lead to success.

Once this idea of self-acceptance has germinated, specific goals can be established by both the coach and athlete and a plan developed for the achievement of these goals.

Ultimately, it is the athlete's determination, dedication, and enhancement of self-image that will be responsible for either success or failure.

It is the coach's responsibility to motivate the athlete to want to change and then to facilitate this change by providing the athlete with a physical and psychological training program that will lead to a greater feeling of self-worth and ultimately success.

THE COACH'S ROLE IN MOTIVATING THE ATHLETE AND IMPROVING SELF-IMAGE

The most frustrating aspect of coaching is to have an athlete who has all the necessary physical ability to become a champion but falls short once the competition begins. The most rewarding aspect of coaching is watching an individual with lesser physical abilities become a champion.

In each instance, it is the coach who is responsible for unlocking the physical and mental potential of the athlete and motivating him to want to become successful.

The majority of research completed on motivation shows that coaches are predominately negative toward athletes. They concentrate on what the athlete's faults are rather than on what he is doing correctly. An athlete must be rewarded for his successes, at whatever level they may occur. He must also be rewarded, accepted, feel valued, and look forward to coming back to each practice session.

The coach can develop and use specific techniques for motivating athletes, not only for competition but also for practice sessions.

The coach must help the athlete to establish challenging but realistic and attainable goals. This is done by setting aside a time to speak with each athlete before the season begins. During this discussion, both the coach and athlete will share their expectations and aspirations for the coming season. Definite goals and strategies for achieving these goals can be established at this time.

A GUIDELINE FOR ESTABLISHING GOALS

1. The goal must be believable and imaginable.

2. The goal must be personal, set by the individual. The coach's role is to help the athlete see new horizons by

assessing the athlete's abilities and then structuring a training program to help fulfill these expectations. The athlete is the one who must actually see the new horizon.

3. The goal must be specific and well defined.

4. The goal must be important and worth working for so that the sacrifices being made are considered rewarding and are not seen as hardships.

5. Long- and short-term goals are equally important. Long-range goals give direction; short-range goals give encouragement along the way as they are met. This will build a personal satisfaction that will be reflected in an improved self-image.

1. The coach must show the athlete that he accepts and cares for him, not just as an athlete, but as an individual as well. The coach must be concerned with each athlete's academics, family, and social life, in order to communicate this feeling of acceptance.

2. The athlete must be encouraged to become a better person. This is accomplished by promoting the idea that there is more to life than just athletics. A greater involvement in school and church related activities will help the individual to become a well-rounded citizen. This involvement will also help relieve the drudgery of training.

3. The coach must accept the realization that each and every athlete is unique, worthwhile, and worthy of his individualized attention, regardless of ability level.

4. The magic of believing must be emphasized. Athletes must believe in the coach as well as in themselves. They must believe that what their coach is telling them will work.

5. No athlete should be downgraded, but encouraged from a positive standpoint at all times. The coach must be able to communicate criticism in a positive manner.

6. The efforts of all athletes both in practice and in competition should be recognized off the track as well as

on. This is accomplished through positive parental, peer, and coach-athlete relationships.

7. All athletes should be given more responsibility in the training process. Such things as recording training performances, helping to develop workouts, and fulfilling organizational roles such as event captain are examples.

8. Participation in the program alone should afford all athletes the opportunity to achieve some goal. That goal should include advancement in status (not necessarily performance) in the activity and within the team structure. Seniority, for example, should be recognized by increased responsibility, and with it, increased competence. This is just one way of showing athletes that they are worthwhile individuals, regardless of their physical abilities.

9. Training performances must yield positive feedback to maintain proper motivational levels.

10. Discipline is a must for all teams. The coach is responsible for administering discipline in an effective and positive manner. Discipline should not be used as a punishment but as a positive way to let the athletes know that their behavior is unacceptable. The goal of all disciplinary action is to help the individual grow and develop a stronger code of self-discipline from within.

11. The coach must be respected by the athletes. This respect is earned by the coach through hard work, dedication to the well-being of the athletes, and willingness to help all athletes in all their endeavors. The coach is not just someone spouting philosophies of training and living; he actually lives by these ideals.

IMPROVING PERFORMANCE IN THE MOTIVATED ATHLETE

When an individual has been trained properly, is working at peak efficiency, and is properly motivated with an improved self-image, then visualization or mental imagery will help him to achieve his goals.

Visualization, or mental imagery, is another term for "mental daydreaming." The difference between "mental daydreaming" and regular day dreaming is that visualization is a structured plan for mentally programing an athlete for a specific performance. Just as a writer prepares a manuscript, the athlete can prepare for competition by focusing on an upcoming competition and visualizing a desired performance in his subconscious mind.

Research has shown the importance of establishing a mental picture; subconscious thoughts can create physical reactions. This occurs when the body reacts to messages sent to it by the subconscious.

If, through visualization, one can picture the perfect race, the perfect throw, or the perfect jump, then the negative feelings about competitions can be minimized and the positive level of consciousness will be accentuated.

The most positive visualizations are in the first person. "I really am relaxed, I really got a good start, I really lifted well off the board." *Thinking it makes it so!*

This technique can be practiced in various locations during different times of the day. It can be practiced at the competition while warming up or by finding a nice, quiet spot, alone. Optimum results may also be achieved by visualizing before bed in the evening or prior to getting out of bed in the morning. Any quiet, relaxing, time during the day can be spent planning that perfect performance.

An athlete should never do a great deal of "mental daydreaming" the night before a competition. This will only serve to physically and psychologically drain him. It is okay to go through the race once or twice, but then relax and rest for the competition.

As the athlete becomes more adept at visualization, a very definite improvement in self-image will occur. He will become more confident that he can meet his goals.

More important, negative thoughts and anxiety will be reduced.

KEY POINTS FOR SUCCESSFUL VISUALIZATION

- Stay relaxed and feel good about yourself.
- Form a mental picture of the action to be performed.
- Be positive about this action and always think success.
- Have a mental cue to focus on in order to relieve the mind of distractions and to keep it on the task at hand. Examples of mental cues may be: "speed down the runway, drive out of the blocks, drive the arms."
- Most importantly, DO IT! When the competition arrives, all the mental and physical preparation has been done. Stop thinking about it and let the body and mind DO IT!

Motivation is a neverending task because of the many complexities of individual personalities. However, if the coach remembers that each individual, no matter what his background or nationality, is to be prized, loved, respected, and treated as a worthwhile human being, regardless of ability, each team member will achieve new and never before imagined success.

7

Developing a Rationale for Competition

Success is the key word and ultimate goal of all athletic programs. Successful coaches and successful programs are more than just winning. They are holistic because they deal with the development of the whole individual.

Success in coaching means helping each member of your team to become better. Because of the varying ability levels, you will have to find competitions where all team members can compete. You cannot expect athletes to train hard all season and rarely have the opportunity to compete. They will lose their desire to continue in your program and will never reach their full learning potential.

PROGRAM RATIONALE

As a coach, you cannot make a decision to concentrate in a certain event because that is where your expertise lies. You must evaluate the overall aspects of your program before making a decision on the areas in which you wish to concentrate. Your talent will play the most important role in this decision. It would be foolish to take all your 10.7 100-meter athletes and turn them into 3,200-meter runners just because you consider yourself a distance coach. It would also be ridiculous to expect a 15.0 100-meter runner to remain a sprinter. Your talent will dictate your strong areas of concentration and this may vary from year to year.

The schedule of events will also dictate your areas of concentration. If you will glance at the schedule of events listed in the next section of this chapter, you will find that it is weighted heavily in favor of the sprinter.

SPRINTS	MIDDLE DISTANCE	DISTANCE
High hurdles	800	3,200
100	1 × 800 relay leg	
4 × 100 relay	1,600	
400		
300 Int. hurdles		
2 × 200 relay leg		

SPRINTS	*MIDDLE DISTANCE*	*DISTANCE*

1 × 400 relay leg
200
4 × 400 relay
Long Jump
Triple Jump

On closer inspection, you will see that there is a great demand for those individuals who are the 100, 200, 400 type or the 400, 800 type. In this situation, you would want to build your program around the 400-meter runner because of the versatility this athlete offers in this particular schedule of events. Evaluate your own schedule of events and identify those areas where concentration will be the most beneficial to your program.

Other events to concentrate on are those areas where your traditional rivals are the weakest. If you discover that the hurdle events are weak in your conference every year because the other teams don't have the time to spend on them, this would be an area to concentrate on for easy points.

SCHEDULING AND COMPETITIVE STRATEGY

Establishing a schedule is a very complex task. Competitions need to be scheduled so that everyone can compete and arranged to accomplish what you want to accomplish at that specific point in your program. If they are arranged in a haphazard fashion, the schedule can have a very detrimental effect on your team's progress.

EARLY SEASON

In the early season, competitions should be scheduled to allow everyone to compete. This is necessary in order to evaluate the progress of your athletes, their ability level, and their response to competitive situations.

For your experienced athletes, this is an excellent time to have them compete in events or at distances that they normally do not compete. This can be done either for variety in the training program, as an experiment to see if they can excel at another event, or work on a specific phase of their race by running another race. This last technique could be used for example with a 400-meter runner. The 400-meter runners can normally be broken down into two general areas:

- The sprinter/400-meter runner
- The 800/400-meter runner

In the first instance, the runner may have excellent speed over the 100 and 200, but lack the basic staying power for 400 meters. You would want to run him at distances such as 600 meters to develop his staying power. In the second instance, the athlete may have excellent staying power but lack the necessary leg speed of a 400-meter runner. You would want this athlete to compete frequently at 100- and 200-meters to develop this speed.

These early season competitions should only contain individual events. Eliminate the relays because it is very hard to evaluate athletes running in relays. You may want to add some odd-distance events in to replace your relays.

REGULAR SEASON ORDER OF EVENTS	EARLY SEASON ORDER OF EVENTS
High Hurdles	
100	
1,600	
4 × 100 relay	Substitute 300
400	
300 Hurdles	
800	
Medley Relay	Substitute 600
200	
3,200	
4 × 400 relay	Substitute 1320

REGULAR SEASON ORDER OF EVENTS	EARLY SEASON ORDER OF EVENTS
Long Jump	
Triple Jump	
High Jump	
Pole Vault	
Shot put	
Discus	

You can manage these early season competitions more easily if they are on a dual, tri, or quad meet basis. Usually, large competitions require a limited number of entries because of their scope. Limiting entries will only defeat the purpose of these meets. Allow unlimited entries in each event and give the athletes the opportunity to show their stuff.

In some cases, it can be helpful to conduct these meets on a nonscoring basis. This way you can enter all your athletes, let them compete, and not worry about a team score. This is impractical because you are emphasizing track and field as a *team* sport as well as an individual one. Your outstanding athletes compete in these meets to progress toward their ultimate goal at the end of the season. Your younger, less experienced athletes need something more immediate to aim for. Even though they may be improving their performances, scoring points for the team cause is even more important and rewarding in many cases. There are also those individuals who may not be improving but are at least scoring and helping the team cause. This will give them some feelings of success and self-worth and will keep them working hard.

Keeping the previously mentioned points in mind, it becomes necessary for you to schedule competitions with teams that will challenge your athletes, while giving them a good chance to succeed. If you schedule teams that are far superior to your team, your athletes may be overwhelmed and not perform the way they should. If your team is far superior to the teams it competes against, your athletes may develop a false sense of superiority that will affect them later in the season. It is a good idea to schedule a variety of teams in your own team's ability range. Some may be slightly better, some slightly worse, but never to either extreme.

The main focus of these meets is to allow everyone to compete. This allows the younger, less experienced athletes to succeed and improve while the more experienced athletes train for the late season championship competitions.

The more experienced and developed athletes will also need to participate in some larger competitions at this point in the season to receive the challenges necessary to become champions. There should be very little emphasis placed on winning these early season invitationals. These individuals' goals are focused more toward the end of the season, so early season results are not that important. They place more emphasis on competing against other superior athletes. They analyze their performances and revise their training schedules to meet their needs. Early season competition is an excellent opportunity for them to build their confidence by competing against these other athletes. A point to remember is that early in the season, superior athletes should not be overloaded in the larger meets. The emphasis is still on training with periodic competitions to be used as measurements for progress. Overloading athletes in competition will not give you a true indication of their progress.

MIDSEASON

By midseason, your team should be pretty much established. You will know who you want to run in which events when it comes down to the championship meets at the end of the season. There might still be a few changes in your lineup, suggested by injuries or late bloomers, but for the most part you will have selected those individuals who will carry the team.

It is at this point that interest begins to wane for many athletes. The young and less experienced athletes begin the season with a great deal of enthusiasm and high expectations. The early season meets reinforce this attitude because improvement is rapid and the experience of competition is fresh. By midseason, rapid improvement has tapered off as many individuals reach plateaus in their training. This is also the major invitational portion of the season and many of these meets have limited participation or entry rules. They are also very high caliber and only the most experienced athletes can compete without fear of embarrassment or failure. Not everyone can or should compete in meets of this caliber.

If you are to hold the interest of the young and keep them involved for the entire season, you must find alternative competitions at their level. This may be difficult to do, especially if your coaching staff is small and you're trying to prepare your varsity athletes at the same time.

One alternative is to schedule Junior Varsity or Freshmen-Sophomore meets for these young athletes so they can compete against others with similar abilities. If this is not feasible, continue to schedule on a two meet per week basis. Every Tuesday, schedule a small meet. On the weekend, schedule a large competition. The smaller meet is for those who do not have the ability to compete in the larger weekend meets. The experienced athletes can either train individually during these meets, or compete in events in which they do not normally compete. An example would be students who usually run the 100 and 200. You may want to enter them in the 400 on Tuesday, and their regular events on the weekend. It is important that they do not lose a day's training. If they do compete on Tuesday, it would be considered a speed training day and your training schedule should be adjusted accordingly.

Another idea is to schedule a Junior Varsity or Freshmen-Sophomore invitational or championship meet just before the championship portion of the varsity season. Give awards and treat these young athletes as if they are competing in a major championship varsity meet. Whatever your solution, these young athletes need competition at their own level if they are to develop and help perpetuate your program.

The more experienced athletes need the major competitions to help them improve and develop the confidence they need to do well in the championship meets at the end of the season. Their main goal is to train through the midweek meets and do as well as possible in the weekend meets. Your objectives for each weekend meet will dictate how you wish to position your athletes.

1. You may wish to just run several quality times. This way you limit your best runners to only a few events and fill in with the rest of your team.

2. You may wish to go after a team championship by placing your best athletes in as many events as possible to score points.

3. You may feel that you can win the meet if your athletes only compete in their best events and are not overloaded with additional events.

4. You may wish to split your team and take your gifted athletes to a meet while your assistant takes the rest of the team to another meet.

For the most part, these midseason competitions all contain a regular schedule of events. There may be a few times when the meet will be a relay competition only. However, you should not lose sight of the fact that the entire idea behind early and midseason competitions for your superior athletes is to provide them with the experience and confidence necessary to perform well in the championship meets at the end of the season.

CHAMPIONSHIP SEASON

There are several things to consider at this point in the season. You may have a conference, county, or city championship meet before your state qualifying meets begin.

The strengths of your team as compared to the strengths of the opposing teams will determine your philosophy for entering these meets. You need to decide how you will position your athletes. You may be able to spread your superior athletes throughout the schedule of events and enter them in the maximum number of events to win the meet. This is fine if the championship competition is not a qualifying meet for future competition. If there is little chance of winning a team championship, it is wiser to place your athletes only in those events in which they will have a chance to excel. This will help them achieve quality performances without the burden of wasting their efforts in meaningless races. Help them achieve all-conference, all-county, or all-city status in one event rather than having them come in second in five events.

In the state championship qualifying meets there are two premises that dictate the positioning of your athletes:

- Place them in those events that give them the greatest opportunity for qualifying for the state meet.
- Position your athletes where the greatest number will be in a position to qualify for the state meet.

At this point in the season all team considerations become secondary to those of the individual athletes. It is their time to use all they have learned and been trained for to reach their ultimate goal of success in state championship competition. It is through their success as individuals and relay teams that the entire team will ultimately benefit.

The same philosophy prevails to a limited extent as in conference, county, or city championship meets. If one of your goals is to win the team championship in these qualifying meets, place your superior athletes in those events you feel will give them the best chance to make it to the state meet. You may then place them in some secondary events where they will score team points, but where it doesn't really matter whether they make it to the state or not. They will be gradually eliminated as the meets progress.

Those individuals who qualify for the state are essentially competing for themselves with team success secondary. It is through their success as individuals that the team will receive points. If they excel, the team will excel.

In state competition, the best athlete and fastest runner do not always win. The individual who can handle the pressure and has the experience in this situation will be successful. Experience is the key term. You want to have as many of your athletes as possible qualify. Especially the younger athletes, who will reap the benefit of this experience in succeeding years. You may want to spread those athletes that have the ability to qualify but may not have the ability to do well over the relays. Relays are always "risk" events. A dropped baton or a line or lane infraction may eliminate superior athletes before they even get a chance to compete. Unless you have a superior relay team, place your best athletes in individual events and use them in relays only on a secondary basis.

There is a place for everyone in track and field without giving up team-oriented goals for success. You must first determine what is best for each athlete and then how they will fit into the overall scheme of the team. Individual success and improvement will be vastly retarded unless your athletes are allowed to compete as often as possible. Once your program's philosophy, or rationale, has been developed, build your schedule to offer the maximum exposure for everyone.

DETERMINING YOUR AND YOUR OPPONENTS' STRENGTHS AND WEAKNESSES

Each week, make a statistical breakdown of all competitions to ascertain where your strengths and weaknesses and those of your opponents lie. This can be accomplished by listing the schedule of events and the number of points each team scored in each event. This is then compared with the total number of points possible in each event and a percentage is derived. From this evaluation, you will be able to ascertain your strengths and weaknesses and where you need to improve or reposition your athletes to draw strength away from your opponents. In large scale competitions, a list of all your opponents' strength and weaknesses can be charted. You can determine who hurts whom and in which events. You can actually map out the results of future competitions. You may even be able to influence the outcome of these competitions by manipulating your lineup to take advantage of any weaknesses you find.

EVENT		POINTS SCORED	POSSIBLE POINTS	PCT.
TRIPLE JUMP:	Home	14	22	.636
	Opponent #1	3	22	.136
	Opponent #2	5	22	.227
	Opponent #3	0	22	.000
1,600	Home	6	22	.272
	Opponent #1	4	22	.181
	Opponent #2	3	22	.136
	Opponent #3	9	22	.409

TOTAL TEAM PERCENTAGE AFTER TWO EVENTS

HOME	OPPONENT #1	OPPONENT #2	OPPONENT #3
.454	.159	.181	.204

A system can also be created to predict the outcome of dual meets. The first step is to figure out the total number of points it is possible to earn in dual meet competition. As an example, we will use the schedule of events listed previously in this chapter and a 5-3-1 individual and a 5-0 relay scoring system. There are 141 possible points that can be scored. This means it will take 71 points to assure victory. The next step is to list the order of events with your best and worst predictions for scoring in each event. This will be based on your analysis of:

- your team's best performances
- the opposing team's best performances
- how you think the opposing team will position its athletes for their maximum scoring potential
- how you think you should position your athletes for your maximum scoring potential
- how you can adjust your lineup to exploit the opposing team's weaknesses
- how you feel you can adjust your lineup to cover your weaknesses

From this best and worst prediction, you should arrive at an average score or what you feel the actual score and outcome of the meet will be.

	BEST	WORST	AVERAGE
HIGH HURDLES	8-1	8-1	8-1
100	6-3	4-5	5-4
1,600	3-6	3-6	3-6
4 × 100 RELAY	5-0	5-0	5-0
400	9-0	8-1	8-1
800 HURDLES	8-1	8-1	8-1
800	1-8	0-9	1-8
MEDLEY RELAY	0-5	0-5	0-5
200	6-3	6-3	6-3
3,200	3-6	3-6	3-6
4 × 400 RELAY	5-0	5-0	5-0
LONG JUMP	6-3	4-5	5-4
TRIPLE JUMP	6-3	4-5	5-4
HIGH JUMP	6-3	4-5	5-4
POLE VAULT	3-6	3-6	3-6
SHOT PUT	5-4	5-4	5-4
DISCUS	1-8	1-8	1-8
TOTAL SCORE	81-60	71-70	76-65

SCOUTING CROSS COUNTRY OPPONENTS

Scouting in cross country is very difficult, and usually is not essential nor practical for most coaches. There are several variables that make it impractical.

Courses vary in length and difficulty, making it very hard to compare times and performances unless it is a common course.

Teams that do well in large meets may not necessarily do as well in smaller meets. It depends on the top five athletes and their time differentials. Several excellent runners may finish up front in a large competition while the remainder of the team finishes in the center of the pack. They may beat you badly even though you place seven runners in front of their fourth and fifth runners. However, in a dual meet, if this happens the score is narrowed to 29–30 in their favor and anything can happen.

A scouting report may include newspaper clippings of your next opponents' previous meets, the date and time these meets were run, the length of the course, a description of the course, the temperature and weather conditions, and the course record and its record holder.

The best method for scouting an opponent is to compare performances on common courses or in common meets. You can take their times and places, match them with yours, and determine who each of your athletes needs to beat in order for you to win the meet.

In larger competitions, other competitors will also determine how well you do against another team. Some teams will help you and some will hurt you. This also needs to be taken into consideration.

Whatever method you use to develop the schedule for the season, your competitive plan, or your system for planning for opponents, they should be very well organized and systematic. If all facets of your program are well planned and organized, you will be more sure of yourself and others will have more confidence in your coaching ability. You should know what you want to accomplish, how you want to accomplish it, and when you wish to accomplish it at all points during the season.

8

Competitive Tactics and Tips in Track and Field

Eighty-five percent of competitions can be won on ability and conditioning, ten percent more with the proper mental preparation. One percent is allowed for those competitions where the unexpected happens. The remaining four percent are those competitions in which athletes are competing against others of equal or superior ability, conditioning, and mental preparation. It is within this four percent that competitive tactics play an important role. Knowing what to do, when, and how to do it during a race, as well as knowing what, when, and how your opponent is going to run, is of vital importance. The successful use of tactics requires courage, determination, mental resourcefulness, and quickness to take advantage of every opportunity. Here are some important hints to keep in mind when determining tactics before a race.

1. Know your own athletes' abilities as well as those of the individuals they will face. Variables to be taken into consideration are type, surface, and size of track (indoor or outdoor); distance to be run; the number of competitors; their overall abilities; and the specific abilities of the best runners.

2. Judge what your opponent knows about your athletes and their probable tactics. That will determine both of your tactics.

3. All tactics must be flexible with at least one alternative in case the race dictates a change in plans.

4. Once tactics for a race have been formulated, they are only as good as your athletes' belief in them.

5. The individual with the most speed is the likely winner in any race, regardless of the distance run. All tactical considerations should take this into account. All things being equal, the individual with the greatest speed will win.

PREMEET RITUAL—ESTABLISHING A PATTERN FOR SUCCESS

A premeet ritual of preparing for competition is just as important as tactical considerations. In Chapter 7, you read about mental imagery and the psychological preparation for competition. A checklist of what to do prior to competition in order to be prepared to carry out the tactical aspects of the race will help to ease each athlete's mind and facilitate a much more relaxed atmosphere. One of the best ways of concentrating is to have a set pattern of things to do.

DAY PRIOR TO COMPETITION

1. Check shoes and shoelaces.

2. Don't overeat. Stay away from greasy foods and carbonated beverages. (Carbonation causes carbon dioxide in the blood stream.)

3. Get plenty of rest beginning two days before competition.

4. Always eat a good breakfast, a light lunch, and a good dinner.

5. Do not eat before bedtime if at all possible. If you must, make it fruit, raisins, or milk.

6. Athletes should never try new foods or different eating schedules on trips or during the week of competition.

DAY OF COMPETITION

1. Eat at least four hours before competition. Use good judgment in the type of foods eaten, as they have a direct impact on performance.

2. The athlete should report to the dressing room well ahead of time in order to dress steadily but leisurely and to make sure all equipment is satisfactory. The proper equipment appropriate to the weather conditions should be worn.

3. A full warm-up should be done well enough ahead of time to be ready for the event. It should be gradual and opponents should not be allowed to disrupt concentration.

4. Approximately 10 minutes should be allowed after the warm-up and before the event for the athlete to sit down, relax, and contemplate the upcoming competition.

5. Enough time should be allowed before each competition to follow this routine. There may be times when time, weather, or the unexpected will disrupt this routine. Your athletes should be aware of this and an alternative routine established.

TACTICS AND TIPS IN THE FIELD EVENTS

Jumping Events

1. Athletes should always check the general layout of the track before competition. What is the composition of the runway or takeoff surface? How adequate is the landing area? How long is the runway? What is the weather like? How many competitors are there? How long will the competition be? Is there an opportunity for a warm-up? Where can they get away from distractions or inclement weather?

2. The warm-up should begin well enough in advance to allow for three or four approach run-throughs without sweats and with spikes on. This will allow the athlete to make any needed adjustments in the approach before competition begins.

3. If the athlete is jumping in a lower flight, a full warm-up should be done before the competition begins.

The athlete should then alternate between resting and keeping loose until it's time to compete. Waiting until the last moment to warm up won't allow enough time to adequately check and adjust the approach before competition.

4. Sweats should always be put back on after each jump in order to maintain proper body temperature. The easiest way to become injured is to leave the sweats off for a while, cool down, and then attempt a full-effort jump. The sweats should be kept on until the last possible moment before a competitive effort and then replaced immediately.

5. It's a good idea to prepare a shorter, alternative approach, in case the runway is too short to handle a normal approach length. The length of the runway can be a problem, especially with the high school facility. Because most schools compete in traditional meets every year, it is a good idea to keep a chart on the length and surface of each runway. In this way, you will be able to know how to prepare your athletes for each facility from year to year.

6. Jumpers should always be prepared to jump when their name is called. All mental preparation should be made ahead of time so that when their name is called, they will be ready to come down the runway. It can be stressful to "fiddle around" at the head of the runway in preparation while the two-minute clock is winding down.

7. In all field events, mental control is particularly important because of the number of efforts involved. An athlete must learn to take three efforts in the long and triple jumps and then sit around and wait for all the other flights to be completed before taking three final efforts. The problem may be compounded for high jumpers and pole vaulters. After successfully completing an effort, it may be several hours before they are called upon to attempt another height. It is not uncommon for large

competitions to go on the entire length of the meet. Only through experience and actual psychological preparation can athletes learn to turn their competitive juices on and off at will.

8. Long and triple jumpers should be prepared to produce their best effort early in the competition. There is nothing more demoralizing to the field than to have someone put the contest out of reach on his first jump. This is amply illustrated by Bob Beamon's performance at the 1968 Olympics and Carl Lewis at the 1984 Games. After their first jumps everyone else was jumping for the Silver. Also, if a good early effort is not reached, other flights may improve and bump them out of the finals.

9. Long and triple jumpers will be wise to take all their jumps. They will never know when they may need that sixth jump to win. If they are unaccustomed to taking it, they may be unable to handle the situation when it arises. Also, if they continue to pass when they are in the lead, there is a tendency not to stay warm and on top of their game. All of a sudden someone else takes the lead and they are unprepared to respond.

10. High jumpers and pole vaulters should be prepared to make each first attempt successful. If they are not mentally prepared on each first attempt and need a second or third attempt for clearance, it will soon catch up with them in the form of physical fatigue. Needless energy is spent that will be needed later in the competition at higher heights. It will also put them behind the leaders in misses and they will need to clear a higher height to win.

11. Weather, runway surface, and competitive conditions may affect a jumper's approach. If competing with the wind an approach will normally be moved back because there is less air resistance. When jumping into the wind, the approach will normally be moved up because of an increase in air resistance. If for some reason the high, long, or triple jumper is hitting the takeoff point consist-

ently with the *wrong* takeoff foot, the adjustment is made by changing to the opposite foot for the first step in the approach run.

Runway surfaces may also affect the approach. Some surfaces are faster than others and adjustments need to be made to handle them. Runway and weather conditions have a vast influence on the pole vaulter. In the event of a tail wind, it may be necessary to go to a higher flexed pole in order to prevent too much penetration, thus hurrying the vault technique. Another way to prevent this is to go to a higher handhold. If there is a headwind, a lighter flexed pole can be used to help facilitate an easier penetration so that the vaulter will not stall out at the top of the vault. Also, if the vaulter lowers the handhold, it will help when jumping into the wind.

Any time there is a change in the handhold, there will be a corresponding change in the length of the approach. The higher handhold will move back, while the lower handhold will move up. This can be adjusted by, after marking the takeoff foot on a run-through, having the vaulter stand with the pole in the box. The upperhand's hold should be in a line directly above the takeoff foot. This point is compared with the actual takeoff point. The difference is measured and the approach is adjusted.

12. Pole vaulters and high jumpers may run into situations where they have to pass heights in order to win a competition. In the first place, these individuals should begin jumping at a height that is comfortable for them; not too demanding, yet high enough so that they will not expend a great deal of effort at too low heights.

An example of passing a height to take command of a competition would be if athlete (A) has cleared 14'6" on the first attempt, with no misses throughout the competition. Athlete (B) has missed 14'6" on the first attempt and has one miss at the last height made. Even if athlete (B) clears 14'6" on the second attempt, he is still in second place and must rely on clearance at the next height. Rather than expending the effort at 14′6″ and rather than taking a chance that he will miss his next two attempts, athlete (B) may want to pass these two attempts, have the bar raised, and take them at the next height. This can also be done in the high jump.

13. There can also be a situation in which two athletes have cleared the same height in a competition and the judge asks them what the next height should be. If athlete (A) is the current leader in the competition because of misses, he would want the bar raised as high as possible because if neither makes it, he will win. If athlete (B) is in second because of misses, he would want the bar raised a minimum amount to try and take over first place.

14. It is unwise to jump in competition more than once per week. Hard runways and the great physical and mental demands in these events can tear athletes down and lead to injury.

15. All good jumpers should jump against themselves or the tape measure. They must shut everything and everyone out of their minds and just concentrate on the job at hand—to jump as well as they can. If it is good enough, fine. If not, you must evaluate their efforts and training, and attempt to find a way to remedy their problems.

16. Sportsmanship is just as important a tactic as anything else. Athletes should never allow themselves to get caught up in verbal psych games. They should be courteous to the other competitors and judges at all times. They should thank the judges at the end of every competition for a job well done.

17. Athletes should know the rules of their event and how to compete both mentally and physically within these rules to their best advantage.

18. It's essential to have a mental routine to key on before each competitive effort as mentioned in Chapter 7.

19. After the competition is over, it's necessary to review what happened in each effort. In order to improve, athletes must learn from each competitive effort.

20. As a coach, you should ask all your jumpers for their thoughts on their performances. Was there something they did that day or the day before competition that caused either a good or a poor performance? You are not a psychic. You must be able to communicate with your athletes in order to help them.

21. Proper equipment is, obviously, vital. Athletes must be prepared for any eventuality. Essential items of equipment are:

- a tape measure at least 165' long to measure the approach run
- two ice picks. One is placed alongside the runway to mark the beginning of the approach run. The second one is used if the athlete cannot find someone to help measure the approach. It anchors the tape measure at the board so that the approach can be measured.
- two pairs of spikes, one for competition and an extra pair in case the first is ripped or it rains on the day of competition
- extra socks in case of foul weather
- extra shoelaces
- extra spikes and a spike wrench
- a rain suit for inclement weather
- a sweat suit to warm up in
- extra vaulting poles, both higher and lower flexed for weather conditions in addition to others in case of breakage
- adhesive tape to use as markers or for repairing equipment

Throwing Events

The same preparatory stages for competition outlined in the jumping section of this chapter apply to the throwers. Numbers 1, 2, 3, 6, 7, 8, 9, 15, 16, 17, 18, 19, and 20 in the jumping section can be taken, adapted, and applied to the throwing events.

Shot Put

1. The shot put is basically a power event. In high school it is not so much the size or bulk of the individual as it is the quickness and speed of the arm that is important.

2. For added stability in the throwing hand, it may be necessary to tape the wrist or two adjoining fingers. Both can be done as long as they are not connected.

3. It is necessary that the shot to be delivered with a reverse or outside release. This will enable the wrist to be used in the delivery. If released like a baseball where the wrist rotates out and down from the center line, a proper release will never be initiated and injury may occur.

4. The legs are the most important phase of the throw. They create the power to move the shot away from the body.

5. "Wrapping" the body or rotating it away from the center line at the beginning of the put may help in generating more torque at the end of the put.

6. It is necessary to keep the body facing back, away from the direction of the put until the last possible moment. This will aid in developing more torque.

Discus

1. The discus throw is very dependent on wind conditions. Right hand discus throwers love to see a headwind or an east to west quartering wind. Aerodynamically, the discus is just like the wings of an airplane. If thrown

properly into the wind, the wind will pick it up and give it added distance. With a quartering wind, most right hand throwers will release the discus to the out of bounds side of the right boundary line. The wind will lift it, hooking it back into the sector where it will land just in bounds. This will allow the discus to travel a longer distance.

2. When throwing into the wind, the nose of the discus must be kept down at release to minimize the drag as long as possible.

3. At the release, a strong rotation must be imparted to the discus by the wrist in addition to a strong pull with the index finger. These will both prolong its stability in the air.

4. The discus is released from the first knuckle of the index finger. This gives it gyroscopic potential.

5. In order to keep the nose of the discus down, it is necessary to keep the thumb down on the discus. If the thumb turns up the discus will lose its gyroscopic potential and stability.

6. The discus is "slung," not thrown. It is essential that the athlete let the legs and hips generate the torque to sling the discus and not throw it.

Javelin

1. The javelin is also affected by wind conditions. A tail wind is fine, a headwind better, and a cross wind disastrous. It is best to throw into the wind.

2. When throwing into the wind it is necessary to keep the nose of the javelin down for greater stability.

3. It is important to concentrate on throwing "through" the point of the javelin to gain more velocity and to prevent injury to the elbow.

4. The faster the athlete can run and the farther he can keep his hips away from the rear foot at the moment of planting, the more power he will generate in the throw.

TACTICS AND TIPS FOR THE RUNNING EVENTS

Sprints and Relays

Many coaches ask, "How can you use tactics in a sprint event? You are either fast or you are not." There are a number of tips that will help you give your sprinters the edge they need to win.

The Start

Before the start of the race, the athlete should always check the starter to see just how the competitors are being held before the gun. Is it a fast gun, a slow gun, or does the starter vary with each race to keep the competitors honest. Know the starter.

In the "set" position, the athlete should be concentrating on what the body action will be when the gun goes off. Not on the gun itself. If he pictures the proper movements, they will happen in reaction to the sound. If he concentrates on the gun alone, the reaction will be slower.

100 Meters

In a short sprint of 100 meters, it isn't necessarily the person with the quickest start who will win; the individual whose start places him in the best sprinting position will have the advantage. It is a scientific fact that it takes between 5 to 6 seconds to reach maximum speed. Generally speaking, no one can accelerate after 60 meters if he is sprinting all out. Once maximum speed is reached, it can only be held for a period of 20 to 50 meters, depending on the individual's level of development. A great sprinter is an individual who, after accelerating to full speed, can relax and maintain that speed to the finish line. When it looks as if someone shifts into another gear at 60 meters and blows everyone away in reality that individual is maintaining his speed to the finish line while everyone else is tying up. A sprinter should always sprint five meters beyond the finish line to prevent slowing down at the tape.

200 Meters

Most track and field facilities start the 200 on the turn and finish with a long straight away. Because it is to a sprinter's advantage to run as straight as possible, it is important to set the blocks so that the center bar is aimed at a point approximately 6 inches from the inside of the lane line. The normal starting line cannot be used because the blocks are set at an angle. If it were, the legs would be facing at an angle toward the inside of the lane and the upperbody would be facing down the center of the lane. In order to compensate for this, the blocks should be placed within approximately four inches of the starting line. The right hand will be on the line with the left hand approximately 4 inches back.

Ideally, the sprinter should run as close to the inside of the lane line as possible, but not so close that he has to worry about stepping on or over the line. This is important in sprinting because if an athlete runs two turns in the 400 meters six inches from the line, approximately 39 inches or one meter is added to the length of the race.

Staying close to the line on the turn is accomplished by leaning into the turn. The inside arm and shoulder are dropped slightly, while the outside arm is driven slightly across the body's center line.

Ideally, the 200-meter sprinter should attack the turn at full speed. Once out of the turn, concentration should be on correct body mechanics and maintaining to the finish line. Usually the individual who comes out of the turn in first place will win the race—*if* the proper training has been done. The pressure is always on the individual who is trying to run someone down, not on the leader.

400 Meters

The best method of running the 400 meters varies according to the ability of the athlete. When first learning the event, it is advisable to set a pace that will lead to successful competition in the race and will create an interest in running it again.

Ideally, the 400-meter sprinter will explode out of the blocks and build to maximum acceleration in the first 70 meters to establish position. At this point the athlete should attempt to relax and maintain his tempo. He must make a conscious effort to settle down and work on maintaining correct sprinting technique. At this point in the race, the athlete should feel a tremendous power source from within that he can unleash at any moment.

At the 200-meter mark, the athlete changes gears by exploding again to build maximum acceleration. This is the most important phase in the race and is usually the point at which the race is either won or lost.

When the athlete reaches the point at which acceleration ceases, the race becomes a fight to relax and maintain body form to the finish line. At this stage in the race, it is important that the athlete:

- move the arms vigorously
- maintain proper body lean
- keep the head down, not let it fall back
- pick up the knees
- maintain a relaxed sprinting technique
- drive to the finish line

The most efficient method of sprinting 400 meters is to run as close to even splits as possible. This will allow the athlete to conserve as much energy as possible and distribute it evenly over the entire race. Even though this is the most efficient way, it is psychologically the most nerve shattering. More often than not, the other runners in the race will run a very fast first 200 and the even-pace athlete will feel blown away. It takes a great deal of confidence to settle back and not go with the early leaders. The key to effective 400 sprinting is the ability to change gears (speed) at will, in a smooth and relaxed manner.

SPRINT RELAY RACING
4 × 100 RELAY
THE USE OF CHECKMARKS

Checkmarks are used to ensure a smooth, quick exchange within the exchange zone. Poor exchanges usually occur because the outgoing runner starts too early, too late, too fast, or too slow. The incoming runner will then run up on and sometimes over the outgoing runner, or else be left behind, unable to catch up. The checkmark will assure the outgoing runner of the correct starting distance for a good exchange. This mark may either be made by placing tape on the track, or by making a scratch line on a cinder or crushed brick track.

There are various formulas that have been developed to use in establishing checkmarks. The best method, however, is trial and error because each athlete is different and, therefore, no one method will work for everyone.

FACTORS GOVERNING THE CHECKMARK
DISTANCE

- the faster the incoming runner, the farther away the checkmark
- the slower the outgoing runner, the farther away the checkmark
- the slower the incoming runner, the closer the checkmark
- the faster the outgoing runner, the closer the checkmark
- when the incoming runner is fast and the outgoing runner is a fast starter, the closer the checkmark
- the average distance for most checkmarks in the 4 × 100 relay is 5-7 meters

- in the 4 × 200 relay, checkmarks should be placed at 2/3 the distance of the 4 × 100 meter relay.

PASSING THE BATON

The baton is handed off alternately from hand to hand. (#1 right hand, #2 left, #3 right, #4 left). The baton remains in the hand it is received in.

KEY POINTS IN THE SPRINT EXCHANGE

Receiver

- takes off as fast as possible when the incoming runner reaches the checkmark
- stays to the outside half of the lane if receiving the baton in the left hand and to the inside half if receiving with the right hand. This allows the exchange to be made over the shortest distance and creates an alleyway for the incoming runner to avoid running over the outgoing runner or running out of the lane
- sprints all the way through the zone
- on command, reaches back for the hand-off
- doesn't search for the baton. The hand remains a steady target.
- does not look back
- takes the baton away from the incoming runner
- slows down if the end of the zone is near and he still has not received the baton
- does not switch hands after receiving the baton
- if there is not enough baton to hand-off with after receiving it, it must be gradually worked up by using the fingers of the hand it is held in while sprinting.

Passer

- does not slow down while passing.
- gives the verbal command as soon as the baton is ready to be passed.
- completes the pass as quickly as possible.
- sprints all the way through the zone to make the hand-off.
- stays to the inside of the lane when handing the baton off with the right hand and to the outside when handing off with the left hand.
- makes sure the baton is placed in the proper position for the exchange.
- gives the receiving runner only 1/3 of the baton.
- is responsible for the success of the exchange.
- has the responsibility of yelling either "faster" or "slow down" to the outgoing runner, depending on that individual's type of takeoff.
- does not just let go of the baton. Makes sure it is taken away by the outgoing runner.

4 × 400 Meter Relay

Checkpoints are not usually used in this race because the incoming runner is generally fatigued and has trouble judging when to take off because of this. The outgoing runner must judge the strength of the incoming runner and time the takeoff accordingly, using a visual exchange.

Visual Exchange

As the incoming runner comes in, the outgoing runner leaves. On the verbal command from the incoming runner, the outgoing runner turns his head back and extends his left arm back with the palm of the hand open and the thumb pointing up. The incoming runner has the baton up where it can be taken by the outgoing runner.

KEY POINTS IN THE VISUAL EXCHANGE

Receiver

- always faces to the inside of the track when receiving the baton to avoid trouble from other athletes breaking to the inside. It is also easier for the outgoing runner to see when and where to break when facing to the inside.
- receives the baton with the left hand. It may be switched to the right hand after getting out of traffic.
- takes the baton away from the incoming runner.
- keeps the receiving hand steady so the pass will be made smoothly.
- stays to the outside of the lane to give the incoming runner an alleyway to run through.
- must judge the speed of the incoming runner and adjust the takeoff accordingly.

Passer

- even though exhausted, must sprint through the zone.
- gives the verbal command as soon as the baton is ready to be passed.
- makes the pass as quickly as possible.
- always hands the baton off with the right hand.
- stays to the inside half of the lane when passing.
- stays and coasts down in the lane after exchange. Then stops and looks around before leaving the track to avoid interference.
- makes sure the receiver takes the baton away, does not just let go of it.

SELECTING RELAY PERSONNEL AND RACING STRENGTH

Use these guidelines to select relay runners and plan the race.

1. What is the length of the race and how do the individuals fit into it? Does each individual have the body build, the stamina, the desire, and the confidence to run the race you want him to run?

2. The athletes must work together. Psychologically they must have confidence in one another to generate the chemistry necessary for success.

3. Is curve running important for the race or would straight away running be better? Can an individual execute these techniques correctly?

4. How do the runners handle the baton? Do they receive it better in the right or the left hand? Is it better for one individual to lead off and not receive the baton at all?

5. Who is the best out of the blocks to start the relay?

6. Do individuals run best from the front or from behind? Must they use the competitors' pace to judge their own?

7. The distance run during any one relay will determine where individuals are placed. You may want your fastest runners on the longest part of the relay.

8. How consistent is each athlete?

9. How competitive is each athlete?

10. Do the athletes have the speed to run the race you want?

11. Always look for experience. If everything else is close to equal, go with the experienced runner.

4 × 100 RELAY

This is a very short, competitive race. In most cases, handoffs determine the winner. In this race, each person's leg will be determined by the location of the start-finish line. Is it at the beginning of the turn or in the middle of the straight away?

Usually the total distance run is as follows.

LEADOFF: 104 meters
SECOND: 123 meters
THIRD: 123 meters
ANCHOR: 119 meters

This will vary according to how far back in the acceleration zone each person is placed and where the baton is exchanged within the zone.

LEADOFF LEG: This is the best person out of the blocks who can accelerate well and has the strength and relaxation to maintain.

SECOND LEG: This is the fastest runner. Placed as far back in the acceleration zone as possible, this person will run the longest leg. He should be a great straight away sprinter. This is the individual who will break the race open.

THIRD LEG: This athlete is placed inside the exchange zone. He must be able to accelerate into the turn and run it technically correct, with reckless abandon.

ANCHOR LEG: This runner is the best competitor. He must be fast enough to come from behind in a close race and tough enough to hold off all challenges coming into the finish.

Very rarely will the anchor leg be able to come from behind to win in a championship competition. The race is almost always won or lost on the first three legs. It is best to break the race open on the second and third legs. This puts the pressure on the other teams to catch up and they may press themselves into mistakes.

4 × 200

Handoffs are not as crucial in this relay as in the 4 × 100. Checkmarks are placed at two-thirds the distance of the shorter relay. By placing each athlete halfway back into the acceleration zone, each individual will receive the baton approximately in the middle of the zone. This allows each person to run 200 meters. If you have the strong 200-400 sprinter on the end of the relay, you may want that person to run a longer leg.

LEADOFF LEG: This is a good starter who is strong enough to accelerate quickly and give you position from the gun. He must be able to run a strong open 200 in order to give you a good first split.

SECOND LEG: Your weakest athlete should run in this spot. He must be able to maintain the position gained by the leadoff runner.

THIRD LEG: This is the most crucial leg of the race. This athlete must be able to break the race open or get the team back into contention. Either your fastest athlete or your best competitor should run this leg.

ANCHOR LEG: This should be your fastest athlete. He must have the ability to come from behind or to hold on to the lead.

4 × 400

It is important to maintain contact with the leaders at all points during this race. The leadoff leg is vital for maintaining this contact. If you fall behind early, the remaining three athletes will have to swing wide to pass and will lose valuable time and distance.

LEADOFF LEG: Make this a good, steady runner, one who may have trouble running alone, up front, and competes best when head-up with another runner. He does not necessarily have to be one of your fastest runners, but he must always bring you into contention.

SECOND LEG: This should be your second fastest athlete. He should have the ability to break open the race or come from behind to get back into contention, and should be a quick accelerator who can move to the inside advantage quickly after the handoff.

THIRD LEG: Place an outstanding competitor here, one who has the ability to hold the lead and fight off constant attacks from behind. He must also have the ability to keep your anchor leg in the race.

ANCHOR LEG: This individual should have the desire and ability to break the field if ahead, or run down those in front, if behind. He must be extremely calm under pressure and have that "win at all cost" attitude no matter what the situation. Once a move has been made, the athlete must have the intestinal fortitude to keep attacking, no matter how long it takes to overcome a challenge from another competitor—even if it means passing on the turn. Once a move has been made the athlete shouldn't back off.

In the 4 × 400 relay, when runners have broken to the inside, the leader may be challenged at some point. This usually occurs on the backstretch where there is plenty of straight away to pass. Most runners are reluctant to pass on the turn because of the added distance and wasted energy. If other runners are passing on the backstretch, the leader should speed up just enough to hold the challengers off. If your runners are challenging the leader, once they make the move they should continue, even if it means going into the turn. It is hard to make a move, slow down, and then make a move again in the 400. An athlete should begin accelerating half way through the turn and jump the leader as soon as he hits the straight away if he is making a move on the final turn.

It is a good idea to establish a running order early in the season for the athletes to become accustomed to one another. Once an order has been established, stick with it. It is very dangerous to change in mid or late season. It can throw off the entire rhythm of the relay.

Include alternates in your practices in case someone becomes injured. Make sure all your relay members know the rules of their event.

HURDLERS

Good hurdlers are those individuals who concentrate on their own races and do not worry about what others are doing. This only distracts them. They should approach the race as if they are the only ones in it. The greatest error a hurdler can make is to look around at the other competitors. This distraction and loss of concentration can lead to hitting the hurdles and possible disaster.

An intermediate hurdler encounters additional problems. The shortest distance on the turn is to run the curve as tightly as possible. It is very difficult to do this unless you have a left leg lead. If a right leg lead is used, the hurdler has a tendency to "hook" (not clear) the trail leg. It is necessary for this hurdler to make adjustments by running more to the center or outside center of the lane.

The majority of intermediate hurdlers take 15 strides between hurdles. The good ones will run 13 strides for the first 4 or 5 hurdles and then cut back to 15 for the remaining ones because of fatigue. When a change becomes necessary, it should be effected smoothly and quickly after clearing a hurdle. The change should be made by shortening the stride and quickening the tempo. If the hurdler can alternate legs effectively it is easy to run a 14–15 stride pattern.

MIDDLE DISTANCE AND DISTANCE

Regardless of the length of the race, it comes down to who is the fastest at the end. Speed rules. It is common in track and field to take those who do not have speed and move them up to a longer distance. The slower the person, the longer the distance. The great middle distance and distance runners of today have disproved this theory. Seb Coe, Steve Ovett, Steve Cram, and Jocquim Cruz are all capable of running 46 in the 400. If they can stay close to the pace for the first portion of the race, their speed will win in the end.

When you are setting the pace, it is extremely difficult to maintain. Other runners can relax and just follow while the leader must absorb mental and physical stress to lead. The leader has a tendency to back off about one-third into the race, because of fatigue and in preparation for the final sprint. This is normally when the rest of the pack begins to catch up. In the mile, it is the third 400 and in the 800, the third 200 that causes the problems. At this point, the athlete needs to make a conscious effort to speed up. It is also an excellent time to break the race open because others are slowing down. If the runner builds enough of a lead, the kickers may not be able to run the leader down.

It is a good idea to follow an even pace for maximum physiological efficiency and relaxation. This will also lead to fast times because the athlete is running economically and not incurring a large oxygen debt at the beginning of the race. However, it is very difficult to do this. In actual competition, excess nervous energy and a fight for position almost always mean a fast pace in the beginning of the race. A large group of competitors may also mean that the elite athletes have to break away early in order to avoid trouble. It may also be necessary to vary the pace because of the other competitors. There may be a strong finisher and the only way to beat that person is to set a fast pace in the beginning to neutralize the sprint at the end.

In most outdoor distance races, the leader after the first 800 has usually gone out too fast. It is wise to settle back at a relaxed pace and wait for the final third of the race to begin making a move to the front. The other athletes usually show signs of fatigue at this point and it is easier to challenge them. An athlete must remain in contact with the leaders if a late race challenge is to be successful. What happens far too often is that athletes allow themselves to fall off the pace and lose contact with the leaders. They will either be running by themselves or with a much slower group. When this happens, the pace continues to get slower and slower and they continue to fall farther and farther behind as they begin racing their group and not the leader.

If an athlete is leading, it is wise for him to pick up the pace when he is challenged in order to discourage the opponent. The Europeans first introduced "surging" as a major race tactic. The athlete follows a normal pace but periodically increases the pace dramatically for a specified distance before falling back into the normal pace again. This enables the leader to break contact with the group in addition to throwing a scare into the other competitors by forcing a pace no one is anxious to follow. It must be noted that surging is a very difficult tactic both mentally and physiologically and any marked pace change can only occur once or twice in a race without affecting the athlete.

To pass, the athlete should move in a very authoritative and determined manner in order to break the opponent. This should be done very quickly to surprise the opponent and gain about a five-meter lead before the opponent can react. The athlete should rarely pass on the turns because of the added distance involved.

Try to avoid having your athletes follow in the first lane. This can be very dangerous, especially in the last stages of a race when opponents may move up and create a box that is difficult to overcome. It is more sensible to trail a half lane wide, staying on the outside (right) shoulder of the leader. This puts the athlete in position to move out and take the lead at will.

Once he is committed to the lead, the athlete should welcome it with a confident and relaxed attitude. This mental alertness is essential to the pace and can only be maintained through planning and experimentation. This includes such things as thinking about the other competitors—their position, level of fitness, and probable tactics and when they will use them. This will keep his mind off his own fatigue and help him to stay alert for sudden challenges and quick decisions.

It is an axiom in coaching that an athlete should never look back while in the lead. Especially during races where the finish may be hotly contested. It is very easy to lose concentration and fall while looking around. If the leader looks over the left shoulder to see where an opponent is, the opponent may be driving from the right side instead. Looking back only breaks concentration and contributes to making errors that are otherwise avoidable.

The most important factor in middle distance and distance running is the minimum distance within which the athlete can outrun the other competitors. If the pace is slow, and the athlete is in control and is faster than everyone else, a final sprint of only 50 meters may be needed. If the race is between a number of individuals with good sprint speed, a larger, more sustained drive may be needed to secure the victory.

The 800 meters is a far more challenging race because of the speed involved. It is almost a sprint as most high school athletes run the first 400 in the mid-50-second range. If an athlete is not in position from the beginning, running wide on the turns and the jostling of the pack will wreck havoc with the pace. It is better to be ahead of pace at the end of the first 400. If a 2:00.0 is the goal, have the athlete go out under 60.0 for the first 400. Very few athletes are capable of negative splits (running the last 400 meters faster than the first).

A conscious effort should be made to speed up the third 200. This is the point where most runners are slowing down to prepare for the final 200. Let the opponent kick first and do all the work while your athlete remains on the outside shoulder. When both athletes hit the straight away, your athlete should make a move to pass and kick to the finish line.

As in all races, athletes should sprint five meters beyond the finish line as added insurance against slowing down.

TACTICS AND TIPS FOR CROSS COUNTRY

Cross country is a competely different aspect of distance running. It is a team sport and the team and the number one runner are only as good as the fifth runner on the team. As a result of this, team tactics are employed at the expense of individual tactics.

Bunching is a tactic in which members of a team stay fairly close together throughout the race. This is very effective when the members of a team have similar ability levels. It is also advantageous to help a weak member of the team to a faster pace. Bunching implies the group will run towards the front of the pack. It is obviously of no advantage if the team is at the back of the pack. If there are one or two outstanding members of the team, it may be wise to allow them to go out on their own and bunch the remainder of the team. At some prearranged point in the race, each runner should be on his own to come home as fast as possible.

Another excellent technique is to match the runners of your team with the members of the opposing team who are of equal ability. You instruct your runners not to let the person they are matched with beat them. That is their only concern.

9

Organizing and Managing a Large-Scale Competition

If you have been successful in selling your program to potential spectators, the next phase is to see that all home competitions are full of color and reflect the interests of the spectators and athletes. Few people realize the difficulties involved in putting on a large scale track and field competition.

OFFICIALS

A competition cannot be managed smoothly without an adequate number of well-trained officials to cover all of the events. If the officials do not know what they are doing, you are better off not having them. Unlike other sports where certified officials are hired to officiate a contest, most track and field competitions have to rely on untrained volunteers from within the school and community as officials. These individuals are usually other coaches on the staff, faculty volunteers, parents, former track athletes, Booster Club members, and interested community members. Wherever they come from, they need to be trained to adequately handle their responsibilities as efficiently and decisively as possible.

The first step is to have an interested officials meeting one evening before the season begins. This can be held in conjunction with a Booster's meeting. This meeting is not intended to bring together and organize officials. It is to prepare to have a well-planned and efficient organizational meeting. At this meeting, you will set the agenda for the organizational meeting and decide on the best methods for advertising it. At this time a committee is established to:

1. Contact by mail or phone all previously involved officials.

2. Place a notice in the local press media of the date, place, and time for the organizational meeting and who is to be contacted concerning this meeting.

3. Place notices in the teachers mail boxes or post information in the teachers lounge.

4. Encourage each person attending to bring one or more interested friends.

The organizational meeting is to give a general overview of the meets during the upcoming season and to give each person a basic understanding of each track and field event. This can be accomplished by showing the rules film on high school track and field. This is entitled *The Challenge of Track and Field*, and may be obtained from the National Federation of State High School Associations, 11724 Plaza Circle, P.O. Box 20626, Kansas City, Missouri, 64195. Video cassettes or transparencies may also be ordered. This meeting is also used to find out at which events the volunteers are interested in officiating so that future training sessions can be scheduled. Key personnel to be chosen are:

Games Committee: Their primary function is to give the meet director assistance and guidance with organizing and promoting the meet. It is usually composed of the head coach, the assistant coaches, and the athletic director, on the high school level. Their responsibilities will include advice on such matters as establishing a time schedule, seeding heats and lanes, and determining starting heights and order of competition for all field events. This committee will also serve as a jury of appeals if need be, and serve as a general advisory board for the conduct of the meet.

Meet Director: This is the key position in determining the success or failure of a meet. This person is usually the head coach. His general duties are to supervise the conduct of the meet and to do everything possible to guarantee the meet will run smoothly.

Referee: This individual is in charge of the meet and makes the final decision on all disqualifications and those situations not covered by the rules.

Starter: This person has control over all aspects of the start. His duties include giving appropriate starting instructions to the athletes, beginning races promptly after the clerk has released the participants, and making sure that every start is conducted strictly by the rules. An assistant starter should be used to aid the starter.

Clerk of the Course: Normally, the clerk of the course is in a central location, to check the participants in and inform them of their heat and lane assignments.

Head Timer: The person who assigns responsibilities to the timers at the finish line and makes the final decision on all times is the head timer.

Head Finish Judge: This individual is in charge of all place pickers and records, and makes the final decisions on all questions concerning places.

Chief Inspector: Supervision of the other inspectors and the final decision making on all questions concerning their responsibilities fall to this person.

Chief Field Judge: He is the referee of the field events.

Marshal: This official supervises all areas of the track and field and keeps them clear and unobstructed.

Announcer: This is a very important position. The announcer is responsible for announcing:

- lane, school, and a brief summary of each competitor
- jumping or throwing order
- event record and who holds it
- lap splits, the names and schools of the leaders, and whether or not they are on record pace
- the new leaders after each round in field events, and when the leading competitors are up
- unofficial times for each race and whether or not it was a record
- the full results of each event
- up-to-date team scores at frequent intervals
- accurate and timely calls for each event and when and where to report to the clerk

All officials should be responsible adults. Nothing can cause problems quicker than having a student officiating. It leaves you wide open for controversy.

Call on cheerleaders, school club members, and non-participating team members to aid the officials with their events and to act as hurdle crews. A great deal of meet time can either be saved or lost, depending on the hurdle crew.

As all of your officials are volunteers, it is an excellent idea to provide them with some form of apparel in appreciation for their services (T-shirt, hat, etc.), and to distinguish them as officials. A follow-up letter should be sent several days after the meet thanking them for their services.

PLANNING THE COMPETITION

Planning must begin well in advance to ensure a well organized, successful competition. The first order of business is to select a date for hosting the meet. It should not conflict with other meets in your area. Reserve that date on your school calendar so that other activities can be planned around it. This should become a "regular" date so that it is hosted on the same weekend each year.

The next step is to develop a card file on probable participating schools. This information should contain the following:

- name of school
- address, zip code, and telephone number
- coach's name and home telephone number

From this master list, invitations are sent asking the coaches to reserve your date on their calendars for the upcoming season. This invitation should include the following:

- an invitation to participate
- the date and time of your meet

- a form indicating an intention to participate with instructions that it be returned to you by a specific date

After this information has been returned, a sanction may be sought from your State Association to host the meet. Contracts can then be sent to the participating schools.

Approximately one month before the meet, send a follow-up invitation, information sheet, and an entry form to each school. This packet should include:

- date and time of the meet
- general information to include location of the school and track, a map for those who are unfamiliar with your facility, where the buses should park, who may be admitted at no charge, which gates to use for entrance, where the teams may sit, where your dressing and restroom facilities are located, and where to pick up any additional information
- the awards that will be given and the places where they will be given
- the amount of entry fee, if any
- the maximum number of entries allowed per event
- a time schedule and order of events for the coaches meeting, preliminaries, and finals
- an entry sheet broken down by event with space for the name of each athlete entered and their previous best performances. A date should also be included when this information should be returned to you. Also indicate whether adds will be allowed if someone scratches from an event.

Usually you will want the entries returned to you no later than the Wednesday before a Saturday competition. This will allow you enough time to set up heat and lane assignments. Once this information has been obtained, a program can be put together including heat and lane assignments, meet records, and any additional information you wish to add.

The meet should be publicized extensively in the school and community. Run daily announcements in the school bulletin, have the local media run articles on the outstanding teams and individuals entered, and display your awards in a prominent location in the business district. Make an effort to draw as many fans as possible to your competition.

AWARDS

One of the most effective ways to keep teams coming back is to have high quality awards with no entry fee required. To help defray the cost of these awards, solicit businesses, organizations, and school clubs to sponsor an event by providing the funds for the awards in each event. If you have a seventeen-event meet, have seventeen sponsors. If the awards you are giving cost $10 per event, have each organization donate $10 and then name the event after them. An example would be the "Key Club 100-Meter Dash." Give them nice publicity in the program and also over the public address system, thanking them for their support. It's a great and inexpensive way for them to get publicity and for you to provide quality awards at a reasonable price.

FIELD PREPARATION

Every attempt should be made to arrange the competitive areas so that spectators will have an easy time seeing all events. It is useless for the fans to watch the field events from a spot so far away that even binoculars are of little help. These events should take place near the edge of the track where all can see. Finish lines should be planned so they are easily seen by all. There should be only one finish line common to all races. The finish line judges should be placed on the inside of the track so as to not interfere with the spectators' line of sight.

AN ADMINISTRATIVE CHECKLIST FOR THE TRACK AND FIELD INVITATIONAL

Prior to the Meet

_____ Determine the date

_____ Reserve the meet site and facility

_____ Obtain sanction

_____ Invite and contract participating teams

_____ Establish the games committee

_____ Select and train all officials

_____ Send meet information to participating schools

_____ Solicit sponsors for your awards

_____ Purchase the awards

_____ Prepare all score cards and event forms

_____ Invite special guests

_____ Arrange for the training room facilities to be opened and staffed

_____ Arrange lodging for visiting teams if necessary

_____ Establish the final time schedule

_____ Arrange for Premeet publicity to the news media, community, and school

_____ Arrange for ticket sellers, ticket takers, and program sellers

_____ Check arrangements for the locker room and shower facilities

_____ Prepare officials' packets and arrange for a check-in station for them

_____ Make heat, lane, and flight assignments

_____ Prepare material for the clerk of the course

_____ Prepare all field event sheets

_____ Prepare material for the head finish judge

_____ Prepare material for the announcer

_____ Prepare the meet program and have it printed

_____ Prepare a list of the officials' assignments and a facilities diagram showing where each should be stationed

_____ Plan for the seating areas for teams, spectators, special guests, and the media
_____ Prepare the team scorecard
_____ Prepare team packets to include:
    _____ general instructions
    _____ heat and lane assignments
    _____ flight assignments
    _____ time schedule
    _____ meet records
    _____ relay cards
    _____ passes for coaches and managers
_____ Arrange for a hospitality room for coaches and officials
_____ Plan for the coaches' meeting
_____ Arrange for a concession stand
_____ Prepare alternate plans for foul weather
_____ Make arrangements for the parking of cars and buses
_____ Secure the services of an ambulance
_____ Secure police or a security agency

Equipment and Facilities

_____ Walkie-talkies
_____ Tables and chairs for the scorer, announcer and judges
_____ Clipboards, pencils, etc.
_____ Finish lines marked
_____ Field event areas roped off with colorful pennants and streamers
_____ Stopwatches
_____ Tape measures
_____ Starting pistols and shells. (.32 and .22)
_____ Whistles
_____ Two starters' sleeves
_____ Equipment for measuring and weighing the throwing implements
_____ Lap cards for the distance races
_____ Starting blocks
_____ Hurdles in good order
_____ Crossbars (two for each jump)
_____ High jump standards
_____ Pole vault standards
_____ Long jump, triple jump, and shot put toe boards

_____ Extra batons

_____ Crossbar lifter for the pole vault

_____ Distance and height indicators for the throwing and jumping events

_____ Official rulebook

_____ Identification paraphernalia for the officials

_____ Track area marked off

_____ Awards stand

_____ Clerk area marked off

_____ Typewriters and duplicating machine

_____ Rakes and shovels

_____ Brooms for sweeping the circles

_____ Inspector flags

_____ Wheelbarrow for moving the starting blocks

_____ Mallet for the starting blocks

_____ Mats for the throwers to wipe their feet on before entering the circle

_____ Towels for wiping implements off

_____ Check track surface and repair if necessary

_____ Check track drainage

_____ Paint stopboards and takeoff boards

_____ Line the throwing sectors

_____ Check sand level in the jumping pits

_____ Rake and level all pits and throwing areas

_____ Prepare warm-up areas

_____ Clean up the entire area

_____ Finishing tape for the finish line

_____ Check high jump and pole vault pits for safety

_____ Check the lighting and public address system

_____ Secure a video system for the finish line

Day of the Meet

_____ Check in all officials

_____ Hold a coaches meeting to distribute team packets and answer questions

_____ Conduct implement weigh-ins

_____ Organize awards area

_____ Distribute necessary materials to the proper officials

_____ Meet with the officials before their events begin for any last minute instructions

_____ Make certain everything is running smoothly
_____ Start the meet on time!

After the Meet

_____ Check in all equipment from the officials
_____ Secure and cover high jump and pole vault pits
_____ Duplicate meet results and give to the coaches and the
media
_____ Inventory all equipment and supplies before they are stored
_____ Clean up and secure all facilities
_____ Return loaned equipment
_____ Notify news media not present of meet results
_____ Prepare a financial statement
_____ Send follow-up results with thank yous to all competing
coaches
_____ Send thank you notes to all officials
_____ Write down any suggestions you might have for improving
the meet next year

THE CROSS COUNTRY INVITATIONAL

A cross country invitational must also be planned well in advance. As cross country is held in the fall and very few coaches work at their schools during the summer, all preparations should be made during the spring concerning the date and probable participating schools. This is important for coaches' to plan ahead and not substitute another meet. At the beginning of the school year, a reminder can be sent out with a general information sheet to include:

- date
- time schedule
- awards
- course location
- time and location of the coaches meeting
- a course map

- parking instructions
- dressing, shower, and restroom information

There are several very important factors concerning the course itself which will determine the success or failure of your competition.

The course should be challenging but fair. It should include a variety of terrains that will both challenge the competitors but offer no glaring disadvantage to participating teams.

The course should be visible. Cross country can be a spectator sport if the course is laid out where spectators can see the majority of the race without having to run several miles themselves. A facility should be chosen with this in mind. An excellent way to promote visibility is to lay the course out in figure eight loops. Portions of the loops may be repeated but should be of sufficient length so that the leaders don't overlap those runners in the rear.

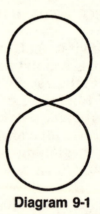

Diagram 9-1

The course should be large enough to accommodate a large number of individuals easily and be easy to follow. There should be a large straightaway at the beginning of the course to allow plenty of running room until the crowd sorts itself out. Sharp turns should be eliminated if possible and there should be a long straightaway at the finish of the race to allow for final sprints, with plenty of room for the finish chute area. It should be well marked with flags and stakes so that runners who are unfamiliar with the course can follow it easily. If possible, the running path should be mowed a little shorter than the remainder of the course to aid runners in following it. The running surface itself should be firm but soft; grass is the ideal surface. Try to stay away from hard roads, loose dirt, and sand for course surfaces.

The finish line is the most critical area of the meet. If the chute becomes backed up, if there are not enough helpers to keep the athletes moving, or if they pass one another in the chute and get out of order, the entire meet becomes a failure. A double chute is recommended for

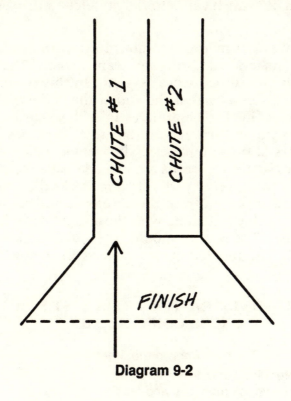

Diagram 9-2

large competitions. Only one chute is used, unless a problem develops and the athletes get backed up. In this case, the other chute is opened and the athletes are kept there until the problem is worked out.

You need to have enough help at the finish line to:

- act as head timer and back up timer
- record the finish times
- determine places in the event of a close finish
- help the runners move through the chute
- aid any athletes who need help at the finish. These individuals may physically aid the athlete through the chute or actually take their place to receive the proper finish card.
- hand out finish cards to the athletes as they leave the chute

There are numerous methods for recording the order of the finishers and tallying team scores. The fastest method is the "quick score" system. In this system, each athlete is given a card at the end of the chute that shows his order of finish. The athletes take their cards to their coaches, who, in turn, record the athletes' names, grades, and orders of finish on a special envelope, along with the total team score. The cards are placed inside the envelope and given to the scorer, who then rechecks the team tally. The names are taken from the envelopes and recorded on the final result sheet along with the official times from the check sheet. The results should be tabulated quickly and efficiently and handed out as soon as the competition is over.

AN ADMINISTRATIVE CHECKLIST FOR THE CROSS COUNTRY MEET

Prior to the Meet

_____ Determine the date

_____ Reserve the meet site and facility

_____ Obtain sanction
_____ Invite and contract participating teams
_____ Select and train officials
_____ Establish games committee
_____ Send meet information to participating teams
_____ Solicit sponsors for your awards
_____ Purchase the awards
_____ Prepare all score cards and result sheets
_____ Invite special guests
_____ Arrange for a trainer
_____ Establish the final schedule
_____ Arrange for premeet publicity
_____ Check arrangements for the locker and shower facilities
_____ Prepare a check-in station for the officials
_____ Prepare a list of the officials' assignments and a course
map showing where each should be stationed
_____ Prepare the meet program and have it published
_____ Prepare team packets to include:
_____ general instructions
_____ course maps
_____ time schedule
_____ meet records
_____ scoring envelopes
_____ Plan for the coaches meeting
_____ Arrange for a hospitality area for the coaches and officials
_____ Arrange for a concession stand
_____ Make arrangements for the parking of buses and cars
_____ Secure the services of an ambulance
_____ Help participating teams secure lodging

Equipment and Facilities

_____ Walkie-talkies
_____ Tables and chairs for the scorers and announcer
_____ Clipboards, pencils, etc.
_____ Stopwatches
_____ Time sheets
_____ Starting pistol and shells
_____ Whistles
_____ Starter's sleeve
_____ Official rulebook
_____ Identification paraphernalia for the officials

_____ Awards stand
_____ Typewriter and duplicating machine for results
_____ Inspector flags
_____ Prepare warm-up area
_____ Public address system
_____ Secure a video system for the finish line
_____ Colorful pennants and streamers for marking off spectator, finish, and course areas
_____ Measure and lay out the course
_____ Mow the course
_____ Check the course for any potholes or other unsafe conditions and repair them
_____ Stake out the finish chute with posts and pad them for safety
_____ Attach pennants or streamers to finish chute area
_____ Chalk the course if possible
_____ Use stakes or posts (4' high) to mark off the running lane on the course
_____ Mark off starting line and team boxes
_____ Identify the mile and two mile marks
_____ Make up place cards for the finish

Day of the Meet

_____ Check in all officials
_____ Hold a coaches meeting to distribute team packets and answer questions
_____ Organize awards area
_____ Meet with officials before they go to their positions for any last minute instructions
_____ Organize scoring area
_____ Make certain everything is running smoothly
_____ Start the meet on time!

After the Meet

_____ Check in and inventory all equipment
_____ Duplicate meet results and give to the coaches and the media
_____ Clean up and secure all facilities
_____ Return loaned equipment
_____ Notify news media not present of the results

_____ Prepare a financial statement
_____ Send follow-up results and thank yous to all participating
teams
_____ Send thank yous to all officials
_____ Write down any suggestions you might have for improving
the meet next year

10

**Improving the
Track and Field
Facility**

In the majority of high schools, track and field is a low budget sport. Very little of this budget is appropriated for the upkeep and development of the track and field facility itself. More often than not, it is left up to the track coach, through fundraisers and donations, to keep the facility in top condition. Much of this improvement and upkeep can be done quickly and efficiently by the coach for much less than retail. This chapter offers numerous suggestions for improving the track and field facility.

FIELD EVENTS

Pole Vault and High Jump

These, like all field events, are areas where safety is the primary concern. A regulation pit with fenders is a necessity in the vault. Of course, a pit costs a great deal of money that might not be readily available. A more inexpensive way to provide a pit is to buy pit bags and stuff them with foam rubber, which can either be purchased or taken from old car or bus seats. Even foam rubber mattresses can be used as long as they are not box springs.

It is important to keep the pit elevated from the ground because of weather. An excellent way of doing this is to either place old tires under the pit or to secure wooden pallets to place it on. Whatever material you use, it should allow the air to circulate under the pits.

Weather, especially sunlight, is the worst enemy of a pit. Ideally, the pits should be taken in each day to be kept protected. This can be a very rigorous and time-consuming activity. In cases where it is impractical to take in the pits, provide covers for protection. These covers can be made of a canvas tarp, visqueen, or some other water resistant material, or they can be actual waterproof buildings on wheels that can be moved on and off at will. (Diagrams 10-1, 10-2 and 10-3)

Something like this could be made quite reasonably if your shop or welding class could provide the labor, while you supplied the materials at cost.

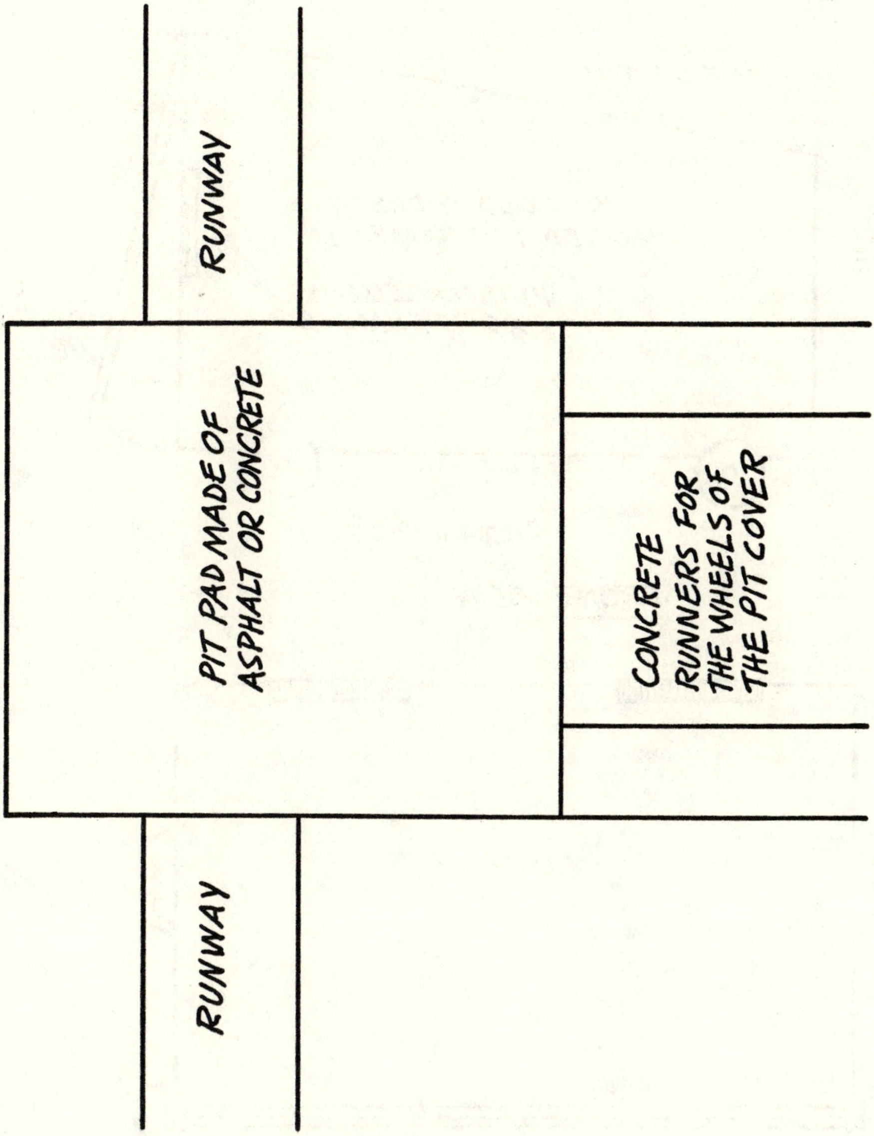

RUNWAY

PIT PAD MADE OF
ASPHALT OR CONCRETE

CONCRETE
RUNNERS FOR
THE WHEELS OF
THE PIT COVER

RUNWAY

Diagram 10-1

SIDE VIEW

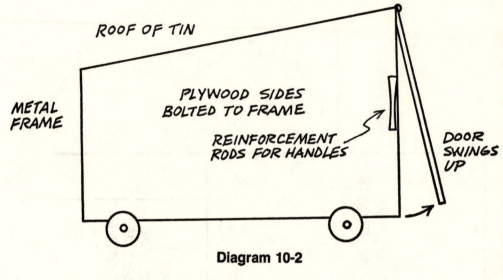

ROOF OF TIN

METAL
FRAME

PLYWOOD SIDES
BOLTED TO FRAME

REINFORCEMENT
RODS FOR HANDLES

DOOR
SWINGS
UP

Diagram 10-2

FRONT VIEW

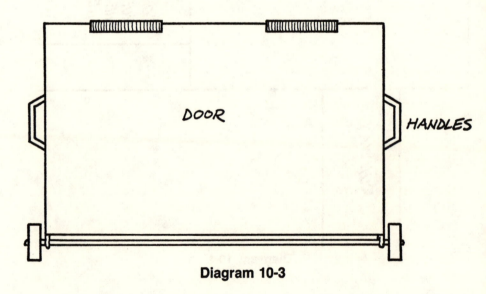

DOOR

HANDLES

Diagram 10-3

Standards are other items that can be made at school for very little money.

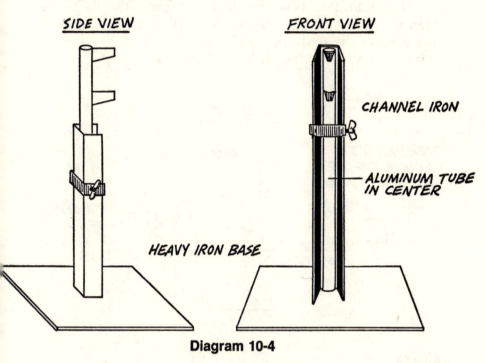

Diagram 10-4

High jump standards are made by first using heavy metal pads for the base. This will reduce the chances of the standards tipping over. A piece of channel iron is welded to each base. Round, aluminum tubes wtih a flat piece of aluminum for a bar rest welded to them, are placed inside the piece of channel iron. Their diameter should be slightly less than the width of the channel iron to allow them to be moved up and down easily. An aluminum shield with a set screw is then slid over the entire apparatus and is used to adjust the height of the bar.

Pole vault standards are made in the same fashion with several variations. A much heavier base must be used to anchor the higher standards. It also must be able to accommodate the sliding adjustments of the standards as allowed by the rules. (Diagrams 10-5, 10-6, 10-7 and 10-8)

This standard is set on the heavy base. The lip of the standard is fastened to the main base by tightening it to the bolt on the main base. The athlete can then adjust it without having to detach it from its base.

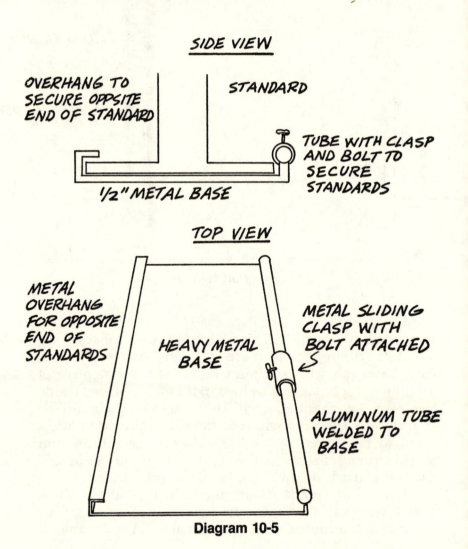

SIDE VIEW

OVERHANG TO SECURE OPPSITE END OF STANDARD

STANDARD

TUBE WITH CLASP AND BOLT TO SECURE STANDARDS

1/2" METAL BASE

TOP VIEW

METAL OVERHANG FOR OPPOSITE END OF STANDARDS

HEAVY METAL BASE

METAL SLIDING CLASP WITH BOLT ATTACHED

ALUMINUM TUBE WELDED TO BASE

Diagram 10-5

Diagram 10-6

TOP VIEW

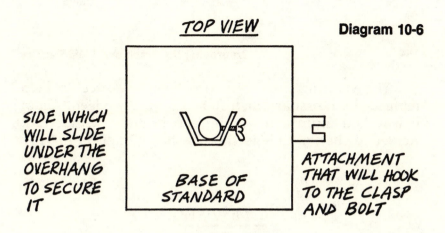

SIDE WHICH
WILL SLIDE
UNDER THE
OVERHANG
TO SECURE
IT

BASE OF
STANDARD

ATTACHMENT
THAT WILL HOOK
TO THE CLASP
AND BOLT

FRONT VIEW

Diagram 10-7

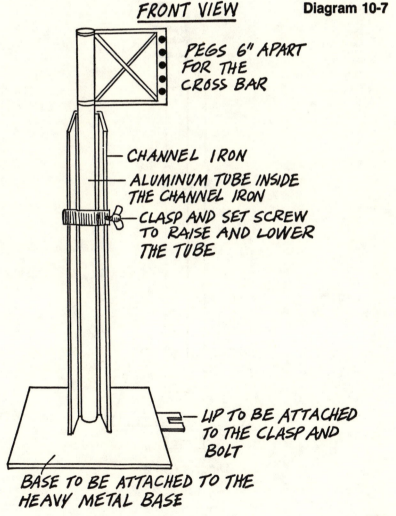

PEGS 6" APART
FOR THE
CROSS BAR

CHANNEL IRON

ALUMINUM TUBE INSIDE
THE CHANNEL IRON

CLASP AND SET SCREW
TO RAISE AND LOWER
THE TUBE

LIP TO BE ATTACHED
TO THE CLASP AND
BOLT

BASE TO BE ATTACHED TO THE
HEAVY METAL BASE

The vaulting area will also need a device to help replace the crossbar when it has been dislodged. Again lightweight aluminum tubing can be used with a fork welded at the top to hold the crossbar. (Diagram 10-9)

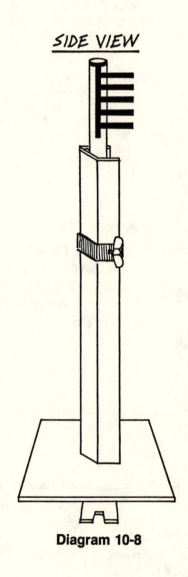

SIDE VIEW

Diagram 10-8

A major problem in the vault is measuring to determine the actual height of the bar. Markers alongside the standards are not always accurate and it takes a great deal of time to climb a stepladder and steel tape the actual

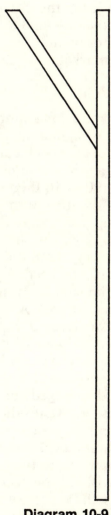

Diagram 10-9

height. There are other, more expensive devices such as a telescoping pole with an internal tape measure. It is much cheaper, and just as accurate, to build your own telescoping measuring stick made from 1″ × 1″ lumber. (Diagram 10-10)

The stick can be set at the desired height. Place it on the runway and move the crossbar up until it reaches the adjustable bar. A high jump measuring stick may also be constructed by either tacking an 8 foot tape measure to a 1″ × 1″ piece of lumber or by marking it at the appropriate heights with a magic marker.

Long Jump and Triple Jump

On the pole vault and long jump runways, 100 feet may be measured and designated on the runway to expedite the measurement of approach runs. This mark can be indicated by painting a white line on an all-surface runway with the number 100 by it. If convenient, lines can be marked every foot. On the long jump runway, the left side can be used for the long jump mark and the right side for the triple jump mark.

On all-surface runways, actual takeoff boards, rather than painted lines should be used. A painted takeoff area will gradually erode the surface from the runway and it will become uneven in that area. A board can be made by nailing or screwing two treated 2″ × 8″ or 10″ boards together. They are then painted white and placed in the runway. A board can be placed at the bottom of the takeoff area to which the take-off board is then attached.

All runways should be edged and the grass kept away from them. If any grass grows up through the all-surface runways or track, simply buy a large hypodermic needle, fill the syringe with diesel fuel, insert the needle as far as possible into the runway where the grass is growing, and release the fuel. This will kill the grass with no damage to the runway or track itself. Do not use a grass or weed killer on the surface if it has a petroleum base as it will soften the surface and destroy it.

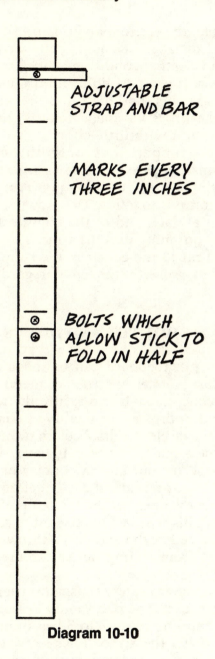

ADJUSTABLE
STRAP AND BAR

MARKS EVERY
THREE INCHES

BOLTS WHICH
ALLOW STICK TO
FOLD IN HALF

Diagram 10-10

If possible, the entire long jump pit should have three feet of a hard surface, such as asphalt, surrounding it. Use of the pit, and weather conditions, such as wind, can cause the sand from the pit to build up around the pit. It is difficult to rake this sand back into the pit from an earth surface. If the pit is rimmed, however, the sand can be swept back into it with little effort.

At many competitions both the men's and the women's teams compete at the same time. This can cause conflicts with the use of the long jump runway, especially if the triple jump is to follow. One way to eliminate this is to have a pit at each end of the runway. Invariably, one group will be jumping into the wind. An alternative is to build a third pit in the center of the runway. This allows each group to go with the wind regardless. (Diagram 10-11)

SHOT PUT AND DISCUS

The shot put toeboard can be made quite easily by your shop class from either wood or metal. It is quite easy to drill the concrete slab and secure the toeboard with a lag and shield. It dresses the facility up to paint the entire pad around the circle in school colors rather than painting a one inch line around the circle. It also dresses it up to dig the shot put sector out and lay in clay or dirt. It can be dragged, rolled, and marked easily before a competition. Permanent sector lines can be laid by pouring diesel fuel on the grass. This will last for the entire season. Railroad ties can be placed at the end of the throwing area to keep the shot puts from rolling out of the area and injuring someone.

You must be very safety conscious when you are laying out the discus area. The pad should be bordered on three sides by a chainlink fence 7 to 8 feet in height. It should also extend down the sector lines several feet. This will keep any stray throws from hitting unsuspecting spectators or officials. Mark the area off with pennants and

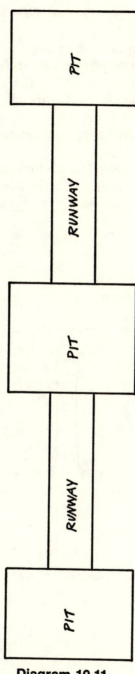

Diagram 10-11

flags to keep spectators far enough away from the sector lines. The circle can be painted as in the shot put area and diesel fuel can be used for lining the sector.

It is helpful to keep spectators informed of individual efforts in the field events. This can be accomplished by building field event progress markers out of plastic plumbing pipe (P.V.C.).

The cards indicating the performance should be made of heavy tag board. Make slits in the P.V.C. to allow the cards to slide in and out easily. (Diagrams 10-12 and 10-13)

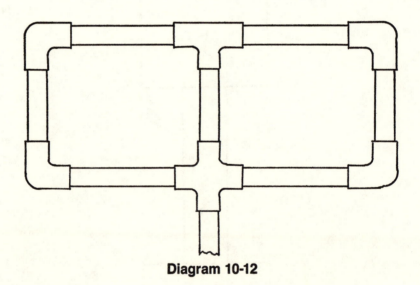

Diagram 10-12

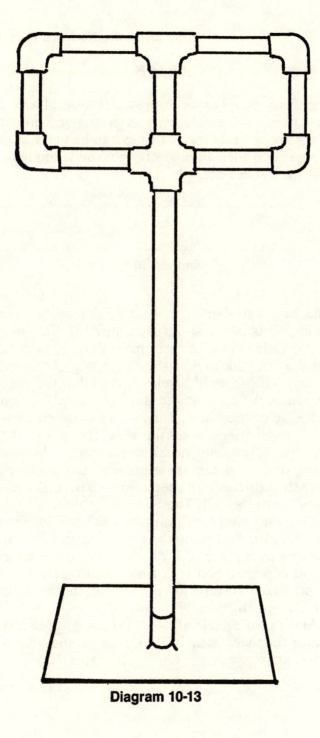

Diagram 10-13

TRACK

The track itself can be improved in several ways to add to the luster and excitement of a major competition. Exchange zones and starting lines can be marked beyond the normal one inch line. Rectangles or triangles can be used to mark these areas better.

Diagram 10-14

The lane numbers can be painted on the track at strategic points, such as at each starting line, exchange zone, and finish line. Lane numbers can also be affixed behind the starting line at the beginning of the straight-away races. They should be elevated so that the spectators can see them. An easy way to do this is to place two poles on each side of the track, run a wire between them, and string plywood markers on the wire. (Diagram 10-15)

The finish line and break poles can be decorated by attaching flags or pennants to poles across the track. This will give the athletes and spectators a better idea of where these areas are located. There are several ways to do this.

1. Cement seven foot poles on each side of the finish line and break pole. String the pennants up for each meet.

2. Cement a piece of P.V.C. in the ground, at ground level, and cap it. When it is time for a meet, remove the caps and place seven foot poles into them. String the pennants from them.

3. Mark your areas with 4 × 4 treated lumber. When it is time for the meet, attach 7 foot poles to the sides of the 4 × 4s and string your pennants. (Diagram 10-16)

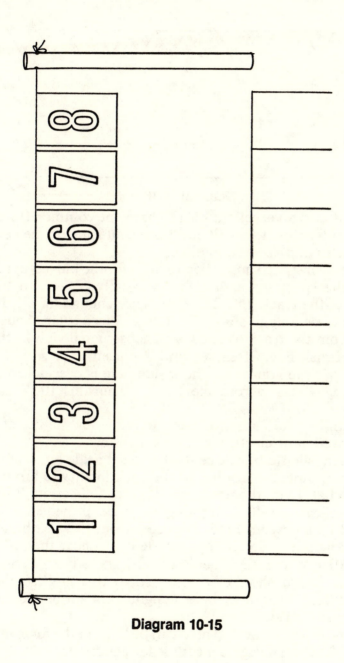

Diagram 10-15

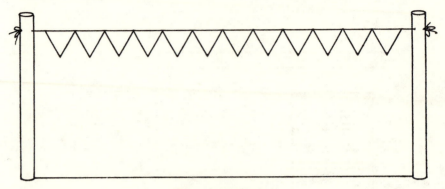

Diagram 10-16

It is also an excellent idea to have one common finish line for all races. This will eliminate confusion on the part of athletes and spectators alike.

A finish stand should be provided for the judges, apart from the spectator area. This is usually placed on the inside of the track. Build a stand large enough for all the judges to be able to stand or sit on it. Place it far enough away from the track to allow an unobstructed view of the entire finish line. Often, a stand is placed so close to the track that the runner on the inside lane is overlooked as the judges scan across the track. (Diagrams 10-17 and 10-18)

Build a platform at the top to allow for the use of a video system or electronic timing system.

There should be one central area set aside for scoring and compiling the results. If the track facility is around the football field, the press box is an ideal location. If the facility is by itself, something must be provided. This should be a covered area, protected from the weather. It should be placed in an appropriate place, near the finish line. All P.A. announcements can originate from here. A bulletin board should be attached to this area so that results and heat and lane assignments to be posted. (Diagram 10-19)

A more sophisticated area can be built in the form of a pressbox with storage beneath it for equipment.

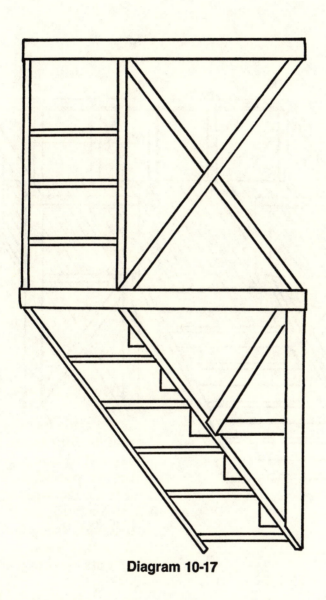

Diagram 10-17

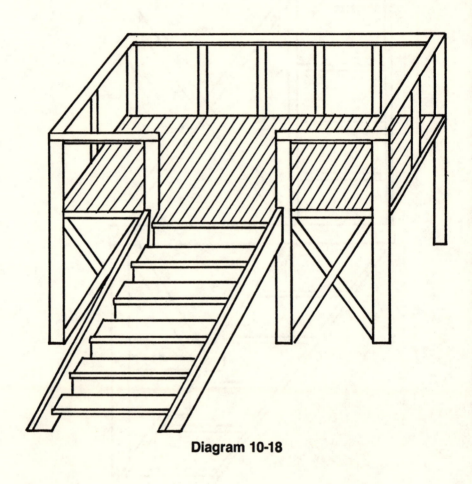

Diagram 10-18

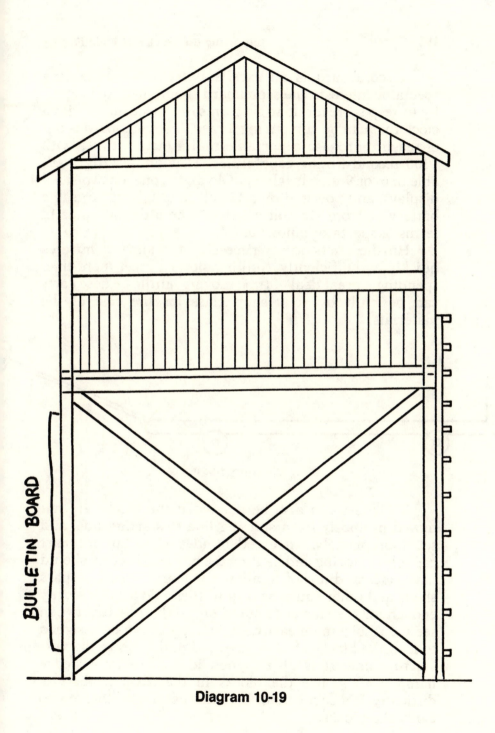

BULLETIN BOARD

Diagram 10-19

A scoreboard is an excellent device for enhancing spectator interest. The scoreboard should have the capacity to keep score for up to six teams in a meet, along with a clock that can be run during a race. If a scoreboard is out of reach, purchase a portable multifunction timer with 1/100 second timing capabilities. They are usually available in 6- or 9-inch bright Da-Glo digits, one- or two-sided displays, and powered by a 12 volt internal, rechargeable battery or from 115 volt ac. It will be a definite plus in terms of spectator enjoyment.

Hurdle carts are a necessity for moving hurdles quickly and efficiently. Nothing slows a meet more than spending a great deal of time moving hurdles. These carts can be built by your shop class for the cost of the materials.

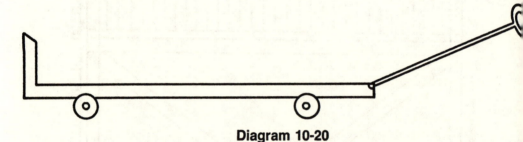

Diagram 10-20

The meet can also be delayed if the blocks are not moved promptly from starting line to starting line, and set appropriately. An excellent idea is to build a cart capable of storing and hauling the blocks. This cart should have sides and a roof to allow the starter to store spare shells and other equipment in it. It should also be sturdy enough for the starter to stand on, so that the timers can see the smoke more easily. An individual can be assigned to load the blocks after a race, and pull them to the next starting line. It is also a good idea to carry a sledge hammer to secure the blocks in the track if there is difficulty. If a cart cannot be built, use a wheelbarrow to carry the blocks.

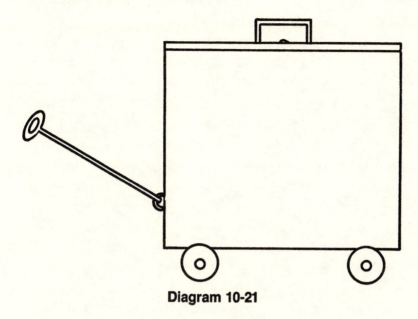

Diagram 10-21

There are many other ways to help dress up your facility that are easy and inexpensive to build. Pennants and streamers for marking off areas add to the color of the facility. P. V. C. is invaluable in the development of worthwhile aids. Make use of your school industrial arts and agriculture programs. They are usually more than happy to receive new ideas and projects. Most of all, be creative and devise your own improvements to make your facility first class.

Index